Perfect-Fit
PIECED
BORDERS

Sheila Sinclair Snyder

Martingale®
& COMPANY

DEDICATION

For Sandy, a plumb line in my life.
I'll love you forever.

Perfect-Fit Pieced Borders
© 2011 by Sheila Sinclair Snyder

That Patchwork Place® is an imprint
of Martingale & Company®.

Martingale & Company
19021 120th Ave. NE, Suite 102
Bothell, WA 98011-9511 USA
www.martingale-pub.com

Printed in China

16 15 14 13 12 11   8 7 6 5 4 3 2

Library of Congress Cataloging-in-Publication
Data is available upon request.
ISBN: 978-1-60468-043-0

MISSION STATEMENT

Dedicated to providing quality products
and service to inspire creativity.

CREDITS

President & CEO: Tom Wierzbicki
Editor in Chief: Mary V. Green
Managing Editor: Tina Cook
Developmental Editor: Karen Costello Soltys
Technical Editor: Ellen Pahl
Copy Editor: Marcy Heffernan
Design Director: Stan Green
Production Manager: Regina Girard
Illustrator: Laurel Strand
Cover & Text Designer: Regina Girard
Photographer: Brent Kane

CONTENTS

ACKNOWLEDGMENTS

I am grateful to have had the support and help of many generous people while preparing this book.

My husband, Elvin, is the reason I can do what I do, no matter what crazy scheme I come up with!

My kids, Matthew and Samantha, and Julia and Spencer, are always interested and supportive, always there with a hug and a little distraction when I need something else to think about!

My little quilting group; Margaret, Yolaine, Arlene, Sandy, Dodie, Carol, Judy, Bev, and Pene, are handy with a needle and thread to help with labels and binding.

My neighbor, Marie Dickes, saved me at the 11th hour with binding.

Lynne Ackerman put her appliqué skills to work and allowed me to focus on other tasks.

Lisa Bee Wilson is a wonderful friend, cocon-spirator, and collaborator. Lisa came to my rescue on numerous occasions helping me to keep things in perspective. She is a superb long-arm quilter! We brainstormed together on designs, and she was able to execute them beyond my expectations. Please check out her blog: towerhousequilts.com.

INTRODUCTION

Have you noticed that by the time you're getting to the final stages of a project, you're starting to think about the next one—or two—or three? We laugh at ourselves when we say we have to live to be 125 years old in order to finish all the quilts we've got planned. That's how I've come to write a second book on the subject of pieced borders.

Pieced borders, or no borders, have been on my mind for several years now. My first book, *Pieced To Fit: Instant Quilt Borders from Easy Blocks* (Martingale & Company, 2004), spelled out my theory that we need an alternative to adding plain borders that may or may not fit with the style or design of our quilt. I use plain borders sparingly. I carefully deliberate what they might add or take away from the quilt design. It's my opinion that we need more choices when it comes to sashing and finishing elements. I've come to believe that these designs can give the quilt a more finished look and make it more interesting. Look at the design called "Swiss Army Quilt" on page 25. If you think about replacing the pieced border with a plain border, the change would make the project simpler and less time consuming, but not nearly as exciting!

I've included a plain inner border in "Stargazing" on page 41 and plain and pieced borders in "Conversation Starter" on page 50. They were used in the designs for specific reasons; to highlight a feature by allowing it to become more prominent in the quilt, or to allow a space for the quilting to become the feature of that area. So, as you'll see, I don't completely rule out plain borders, but I do think through how they will impact the quilt design, and I consciously choose to use them when I think it's the best way to go.

One additional aspect of this book that I hope you'll enjoy and find helpful are the descriptions and close-up photographs of some of the quilting designs. As a long-arm quilter, I love it when I'm given free choice of what to quilt, but I know choosing the quilting design is difficult for many quilters. So, just to get the conversation started, I've included my ideas about quilting and thread color. I free-motion quilt, and then use rulers and gadgets when needed for accuracy, as when stitching in the ditch. Hmmm . . . maybe my next book should be about quilting. There I go again, starting another project before this one is finished!

You'll see by the wide variety of design and fabric choices that I love them all and refuse to be tied to just one style. So, enjoy. Choose your favorite and let me know how it turns out!

I've been using pieced blocks to complete my borders for several years now. The idea originally came to me through my long-arm quilting business. After attempting to teach the quilting world (one person at a time) how to apply borders smoothly, I began to think there *might* be a better way! The thoughts kept percolating away in my brain for a while, and soon I realized that I was designing quilts in my head. They were quilts that didn't have traditional long strips of borders (that may or may *not* fit the quilt), but rather borders that were built of individual blocks.

Here's the thing about blocks: we quilters are really good at making them! The measurements are familiar, the size is easy to handle. We're somehow good enough at getting a "more or less" ¼"-wide seam allowance that we can make blocks that all fit together for the quilt center. So, I say let's play to our strengths.

When you build a border of individual blocks, it's so easy to add them to your quilt. The seam allowances match up, and everything stays flat and square. The final construction of the quilt is simplified since everything fits together. You simply add a border block at each end of the row and the border magically appears as you sew the rows together.

A row of border blocks along the top and a border block at each end of the rows create an impressive border as if by magic.

The choices and variations are unlimited when you consider adding a border to a quilt. There may be some quilts in my future that will have plain borders; those borders are a fine and traditional way to finish a quilt. However, the typical narrow inner border and larger outer border have been seen so often in the recent decades, that frankly, I'm over it for now! I know tastes evolve over the years, so I'm not willing to throw them out altogether, but I'll use them sparingly, and really consider what will enhance each quilt as I'm designing it. What if a quilt is screaming for plain borders—or no border at all? That's what I'll do. I'm willing to do whatever the quilt needs, whether it's tweaking the piecing design, varying the fabric choices, changing the quilting design, or choosing a different batting. I've always thought of myself as producing quilts that are, first of all, functional, just as my Grandma Julia did. Like her, I know that doesn't mean that they can't be beautiful as well.

What I love most about quilting is what I call the "layers" of the design process: choosing fabrics, cutting shapes, piecing, creating appliqué designs, sewing everything together, adding borders, quilting, and lastly, adding a final design statement with the binding. Each layer relates to the others, and this aspect always teaches me something and keeps me interested. While every step along the way can be fun and creative, I think that borders are often overlooked. In your own work, take the time to consider your border options. Almost every quilt can benefit from pieced borders; they make a quilt extra special.

If you think of borders as an important part of the quilt and plan them from the beginning, you can cut them along with the rest of the quilt. Sometimes I even sew the border blocks first so that when I'm finished with the blocks for the body of the quilt, I'm ready to put the quilt together. Pieced borders will change the look of a quilt, making it more interesting and exciting by adding a surprising finish.

Harmony

Pieced borders might be simple and repetitious, giving the quilt a rhythm and balance or a sense of harmony. Harmony is a wonderful thing in a quilt. A design will appear harmonious when you create both unity and variety. Unify a quilt through the use of repeated colors, shapes, sizes, and other elements. Create variety with the contrast of color, shape, and size in those same elements. Traditional quilts get their rhythm through the use of repeated elements in an organized pattern.

Repeated colors, shapes, and size create a simple, harmonious border.

Repeating lines or curves, whether in the piecing, appliqué, or quilting stitches, also establish a strong visual rhythm and are seen in both traditional and contemporary quilts. To take the idea of harmony one step further, I suggest that the layers of the design process should incorporate both unity and variety to enhance the quilt with every possible element, including the border.

designer's tip:
ADD ENERGY

Diagonal lines are pleasing in any work of art because they bring energy and movement to the design. They don't have to be actual lines, but can be the suggestion of direction created by subtle color changes (as in color-washed quilts) or through the quilting design. Take inspiration from nature, which is full of diagonal movement.

Depth

I like to see a sense of depth in quilts, through the use of color or value contrast in geometric shapes. The interplay of quilt patches—squares, rectangles, and triangles—can define the foreground, middle area, and background of a quilt. Sometimes a pieced border will interact and appear to overlap with the quilt body and sometimes it will have a personality all its own.

Borders that interact with the center of the quilt create a unified design.

Random-pieced blocks create a border with a charm all its own. The repeated colors and fabrics, plus the playful mood add depth while keeping it in harmony with the quilt center.

Color places the emphasis on the center of this quilt, while value contrast gives the border a strong presence.

Emphasis

Emphasis makes some elements in a design more significant than others. Size is the most obvious way to suggest emphasis; the element becomes more important because it occupies the greatest area. You can also emphasize something by using color, shape, and quilting. The next time you're at a quilt show, look for quilts that have unusual colors and shapes, not the traditional straight edges. Don't they get your attention and emphasize some aspect of the quilt, giving you something more to look at? Borders tend not to be the emphasis of a quilt but they don't have to be shrinking violets either!

Novelty

You can choose from a great variety of border looks that will give each quilt a personality. You then make it your own by the colors and fabrics you choose, how you arrange the blocks, and how you quilt the project. Sewing pieced borders is as simple as making blocks—because they *are* blocks! So, enjoy the process of making a special quilt. Go with your style, whether it's graceful and sophisticated, ethnic or whimsical, sentimental or artsy. Create a fabulous quilt that speaks to you—from the fabrics, to the blocks, to the borders, and beyond!

A vibrant pieced border adds the crowning touch to this appliquéd quilt.

These fabulous large flowers take center stage, but the borders add visual punch.

A NEW YORK MINUTE

Pieced and quilted by Sheila Sinclair Snyder

Finished quilt: 40½" x 50½"

Finished border blocks: 5" x 5"

Materials

Yardage requirements are based on 42"-wide fabric.

½ yard *each* of 3 medium to dark prints and 1 light print for border blocks

¼ yard *each* of 4 different focal prints for star center and rectangle border**

⅝ yard of medium striped fabric for inner border*

½ yard of light to medium print for star background

¼ yard of dark print for star points**

½ yard of fabric for binding*

2⅝ yards of fabric for backing

47" x 57" piece of batting

* If you want to use the same striped fabric cut on the bias to match the inner border, purchase 1¼ yards total.

** A fat quarter will also work.

Cutting

All cutting instructions include ¼"-wide seam allowances.

From the light to medium print, cut:
4 squares, 5⅞" x 5⅞"
4 squares, 5½" x 5½"

From the dark print, cut:
4 squares, 5⅞" x 5⅞"

From *each* of the four focal prints, cut:
1 strip, 5½" x 42"; crosscut into:
    1 square, 5½" x 5½"
    6 rectangles, 3" x 5½"

From the medium striped fabric, cut:
3 strips, 5½" x 42"; crosscut the strips into
    20 squares, 5½" x 5½"

From *each* of the four prints for border blocks, cut:
2 strips, 6¼" x 42"; crosscut into 8 squares, 6¼" x 6¼". Cut each square into quarters diagonally to yield 32 triangles.

From the binding fabric, cut:
5 strips, 2" x 42"

Making the Half-Square-Triangle Units

Draw a diagonal line on the wrong side of each 5⅞" light to medium print square. Place a marked square, right sides together, with a 5⅞" dark print square. Sew ¼" from each side of the drawn line. Cut on the drawn line; press toward the dark fabric. Make eight.

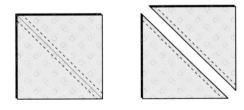

Make 8.

Quick as a "New York minute," this quilt can be made in time for that last-minute gift. Have fun putting it together in contemporary or traditional fabrics. The secret to choosing a good collection of coordinating fabrics is to start by selecting the striped fabric first.

Making the Quarter-Square-Triangle Blocks

1. Using the quarter-square triangles cut for the border blocks, determine a consistent color placement so that all the blocks will be made exactly the same. Label the fabric triangles A, B, C, and D.

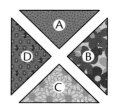

2. Sew each triangle A to a triangle B. Press the seam allowances toward triangle A. Make 32 units. Sew each triangle C to a triangle D. Press the seam allowances toward triangle C. Make 32 units.

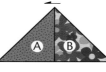 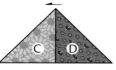

Make 32.   Make 32.

3. Sew each AB unit to a CD unit, matching the center seam as shown. Press in one direction. Make 32.

Make 32.

Making the Rectangle Blocks

1. From the focal print rectangles, determine a consistent color sequence and label the fabrics A, B, C, D.

2. Sew each rectangle A to a rectangle B, and sew each rectangle C to a rectangle D. Do not press at this time. Make 6 of each.

Make 6.   Make 6.

3. Lay out three of each of the rectangle units in a repeated sequence as shown. Sew the units together into a long strip. Make two. Do not press the seam allowances yet.

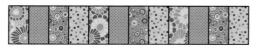

Make 2.

A BIT ABOUT THE BORDER

This quilt has two interesting side borders and three top and bottom borders. First, there's an inner border made of striped squares that are rotated to alternate the direction of the stripe. This border is easy and effective. A top and bottom border of rectangles, half the size of the striped squares, adds interest and repeats fabrics in the center of the star. Then, to play off the triangle points in the large star block, the outer border is made of Hourglass blocks that are the same size as the striped squares. Using one light fabric for the inner triangles and a plain rust fabric for the outer triangles gives the effect of an intricately planned pieced border.

Assembling the Quilt

1. Arrange the squares, blocks, and units into rows, referring to the quilt diagram below for guidance.

2. Carefully position each striped square so that the direction of the stripe alternates from vertical to horizontal throughout the inner border.

3. Place the half-square-triangle units so that the light color appears on the inside edges. I placed the corner units so that the light color was consistent across the top and bottom edges, giving the quilt a more finished appearance.

4. Sew the blocks into rows. Press the seam allowances in opposite directions from row to row.

5. Sew the rows together. Press the seam allowances all in one direction.

Finishing the Quilt

1. Piece the quilt backing using a horizontal seam. Layer, and then baste the backing, batting, and quilt top.

2. Quilt as inspired. The quilt shown was finished with a large-scale design I call Folk-Art Meander. This scale allows the quilt to remain soft and gives it a nice texture. A closer look at the quilting will reveal some hidden surprises. Included are a variety of blossoms, leaves, and other organic shapes. There are also clusters of these motifs and occasional fruits and vegetables!

3. Prepare and attach the binding and label. Refer to "Binding Your Quilt" on page 76 if you need help with this step.

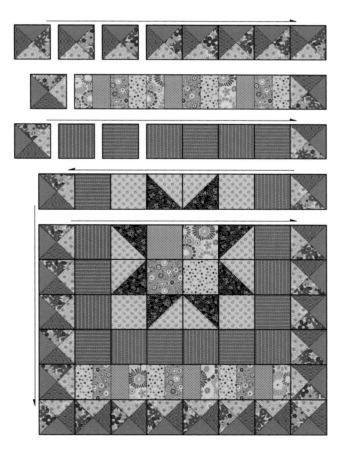

SUN-WASHED SUMMER

*Pieced and quilted by Sheila Sinclair Snyder;
hand appliquéd by Lynne Ackerman*

Finished quilt: 54½" x 54½"
Finished blocks: 9" x 9"

Materials

Yardage requirements are based on 42"-wide fabric.

2 yards of a fun medium-scale floral for appliqués and border block background

1¾ yards *total* of assorted coordinating solids for block backgrounds and appliqués*

1⅔ yards of a light background print for appliqués

½ yard of fabric for binding

3⅜ yards of fabric for backing

60" x 60" piece of batting

Template plastic

* Fat quarters will work here; you'll need 7 to equal 1¾ yards. You can include tone-on-tone prints and any print that reads as a solid.

Cutting

All cutting instructions include ¼"-wide seam allowances.

From the medium-scale floral, cut:
5 strips, 9¾" x 42"; crosscut into 20 squares, 9¾" x 9¾"
2 strips, 8¾" x 42"; crosscut into 16 rectangles 4" x 8¾"

From the assorted coordinating solids, cut:
16 squares, 9¾" x 9¾"
20 rectangles, 4" x 8¾"

From the light background print, cut:
5 strips, 10¾" x 42"; crosscut into 36 rectangles 5" x 10¾"

From the binding fabric, cut:
6 strips, 2" x 42"

Making the Blocks

You'll make all of the blocks in the same manner, but you'll be using two different color and fabric combinations. Lynne chose to do needle-turn appliqué because she likes having a portable hand project, and she likes the soft finish it produces at the edge of the appliqué. Refer to "Needle-Turn Appliqué" (page 75) or use your own favorite appliqué method.

1. Use the pattern on page 15 and template plastic to make a template for pieces A and B.

2. Trace the B template onto 16 floral rectangles and 20 solid rectangles. Cut out the appliqués, adding the necessary turn-under allowance.

3. Center a B piece on a light background print rectangle and appliqué in place. Make 36.

4. Place the A template onto the appliquéd light rectangle, centering it over the B piece. Trace around it and cut out the appliqué, adding the necessary turn-under allowance. Repeat for each appliquéd rectangle.

5. Center the 20 units from step 4 with solid B pieces on a floral 9¾" square. Appliqué in place.

Make 20.

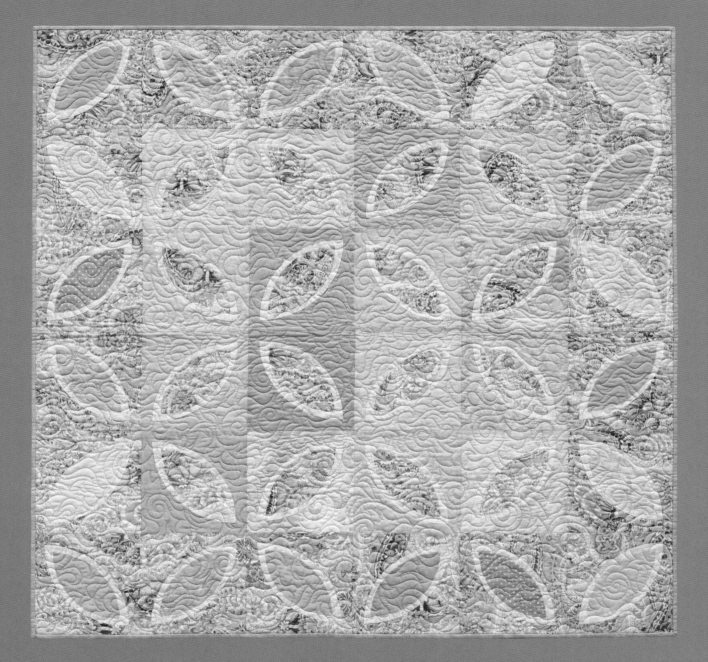

The lovely colors in a bowl of fruit inspired this simple
and portable project. The appliqué is easy and fast, and
it makes a great beginner project. I imagine it on a patio
table set for "Girls' Night In" with a fresh garden salad,
a loaf of good bread, and a pitcher of raspberry lemonade!

6. Center the 16 units from step 4 with floral B pieces on a solid 9¾" square and appliqué in place.

Make 16.

7. Press each block flat from the wrong side of the fabric and square up to 9½" x 9½".

A BIT ABOUT THE BORDER

The border on this quilt couldn't be easier. The blocks are made exactly the same as those in the center of the quilt; only the fabric placement has been reversed. The large floral is used for the background fabric, rather than for the melon wedges, while the pastel colors now make up the wedges. Subtle for a sun-washed look, don't you think?

Assembling the Quilt

1. Arrange the blocks in six rows of six blocks each, referring to the quilt diagram above right. Pay special attention to the placement of the floral and solid blocks; the 20 blocks with floral backgrounds create the "border" and the blocks with solid backgrounds make up the center of the quilt. Notice also how the diagonal orientation of the appliqués alternates from block to block in each row.

2. Sew the blocks together into rows. Press the seam allowances in opposite directions from row to row.

3. Sew the rows together; press.

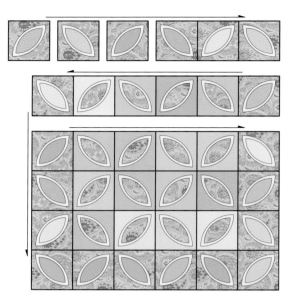

Finishing the Quilt

1. Piece the quilt backing using a vertical or horizontal seam. Layer and baste the backing, batting, and quilt top.

2. Quilt as inspired. The quilt shown was finished with a large-scale design I call Swoosh and Swirl. This scale allows the quilt to remain soft and gives it a nice texture. I chose a lavender thread to coordinate with the colors of the quilt.

3. Prepare and attach the binding and label. Refer to "Binding Your Quilt" on page 76 if you need help with this step.

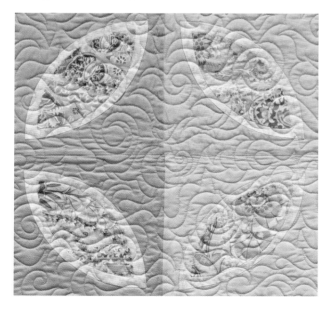

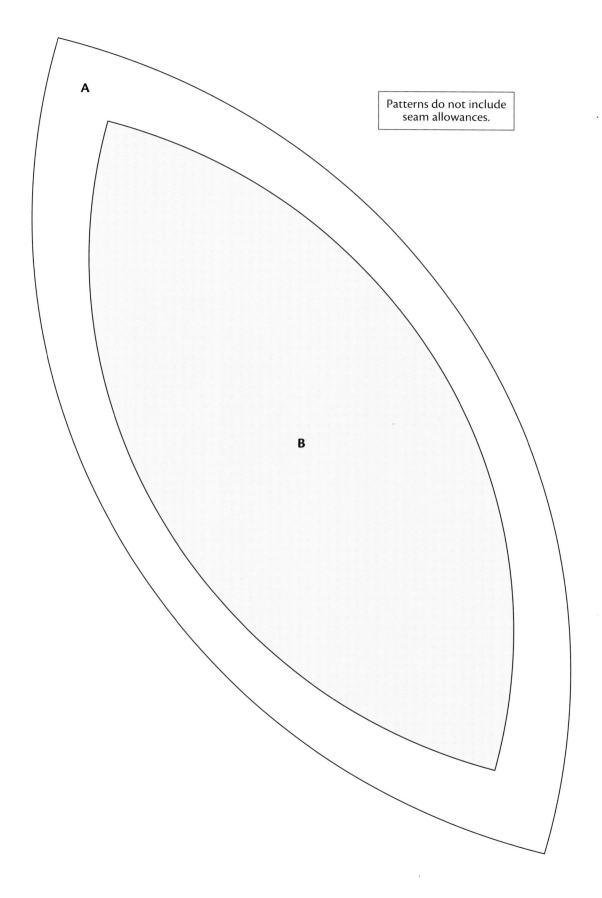

A

B

Patterns do not include
seam allowances.

BLACK-EYED BATIK

Pieced and quilted by Sheila Sinclair Snyder

Finished runner: 19½" x 48½"

Finished blocks: 12" x 12"

Materials

Yardage amounts are based on 42"-wide fabric.

½ yard of black solid for blocks

½ yard *total* of a variety of bright-colored batiks for blocks and border*

½ yard of multicolored batik for setting triangles

¼ yard *or* 1 fat eighth *each* of 2 bright yellow-orange batiks and 1 blue batik for star points

⅜ yard of fabric for binding

1½ yards of fabric for backing

25" x 54" piece of batting

* Fat eighths, fat quarters, and scraps at least 2" x 2"

Cutting

All cutting instructions include ¼"-wide seam allowances.

From *each* of the 3 batiks for star points, cut:
4 squares, 3⅞" x 3⅞" (12 total)

From the black solid, cut:
2 strips, 3⅞" x 42"; crosscut into 12 squares, 3⅞" x 3⅞"
3 strips, 2" x 42"; crosscut into 48 squares, 2" x 2"

From the variety of bright-colored batiks, cut:
134 squares, 2" x 2"

From the multicolored batik, cut:
1 strip, 6" x 42"; crosscut into 2 rectangles, 6" x 14"
1 strip, 9" x 42"; crosscut into:
    1 rectangle, 9" x 18"
    1 rectangle, 6" x 14"

From the binding fabric, cut:
4 strips, 2" x 42"

Making the Buckeye Beauty Blocks

1. Draw a diagonal line on the wrong side of each batik 3⅞" square. Place a marked square, right sides together, with a black square.

2. Sew ¼" from each side of the drawn line. Cut on the drawn line; press the seam allowances toward the black fabric. Make 24 half-square-triangle units.

Make 24.

3. Sew a bright-colored batik 2" square to a black 2" square. Press the seam allowances toward the black fabric. Make 48 units.

Make 48.

4. Arrange and sew two units from step 3 to make a four-patch unit as shown; press the seam allowances open. Make 24 units, varying the color combinations for a scrappy effect.

Make 24.

My little quilting group initiated a challenge to make blocks of bright batiks on a black background. I loved the effect and had this table runner in mind from the beginning. I haven't finished the quilt we were *supposed* to make, but this runner provided instant gratification because of how quickly it went together.

5. Using eight half-square-triangle units and eight four-patch units, arrange the units into rows as shown. Notice that the colored batiks form an X through the center of the block and extend to the corners. Sew the units into rows; press the seam allowances in opposite directions from row to row. Sew the rows together; press the seam allowances in one direction. Make three blocks.

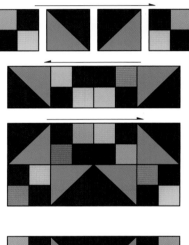

Make 3.

A BIT ABOUT THE BORDER

To emphasize the drama of the quilt center, a simple pieced border of small squares was all this stunning table runner needed. The squares border repeats the square shapes in the star blocks as well as the gorgeous colors and fabrics.

Assembling the Runner Center

The setting triangles are cut slightly oversized to make construction of this project easier.

1. Place a 6" x 14" background rectangle face up on the cutting mat in a vertical position. Cut the rectangle once diagonally starting at the *lower-left* corner and cutting up and away from yourself to the *upper-right* corner. Cut each of the three rectangles in this manner.

2. Position the triangles at the top and bottom of a Buckeye Beauty block, aligning the straight edges as shown. The points of the setting triangle will extend past the edge of the block. Sew the setting triangles to the block. Press the seam allowances away from the block. Trim the extended points even with the sides of the block. Make three block/setting triangle units.

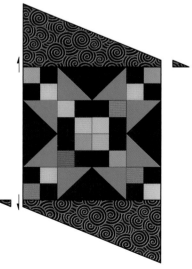

Make 3.

3. Sew the block/setting triangles together into a row by carefully measuring and offsetting the second block 5" down from the top edge of the first block as shown. Repeat to add the third block/setting triangle unit.

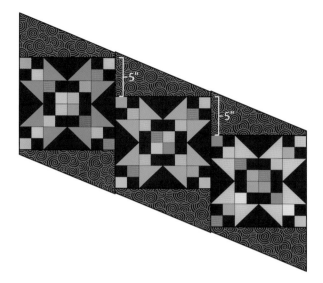

4. Place the 9" x 18" rectangle face up on the cutting mat in a vertical position. Cut the rectangle once diagonally starting at the *lower-right* corner and cutting up and away from yourself to the *upper-left* corner.

5. Position a triangle at each end of the row of blocks so that the diagonal cut edge of the triangle is aligned with the straight edge of the block. The narrow point will extend past the edge of the project. Sew the background triangles to the blocks. Press the seam allowances toward the triangles.

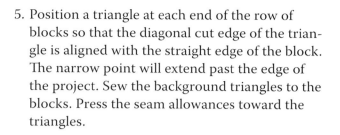

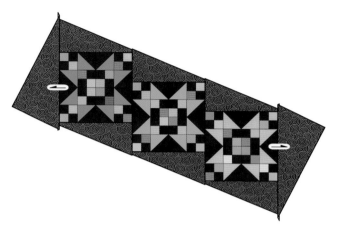

6. Trim the long sides of the unit, leaving a ¼" seam allowance beyond the corners of the blocks to make sure that the block corners will not be cut off when the borders are attached. Don't worry about the exact measurement of the width; the pieced borders will be cut to fit.

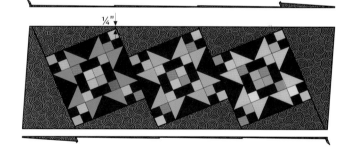

7. Trim the length of the table runner to 45½" by folding the project in half to find the center, and then measuring 22¾" to each end.

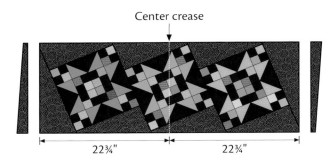

Center crease

22¾"   22¾"

Adding the Pieced Borders

1. Sew 11 bright-colored batik 2" squares together end to end for the short side borders. Press the seam allowances open. Make two border units.

Make 2.

2. Sew a border unit to each end of the project. The units will be slightly longer than needed. Press the seam allowances toward the border. Trim the border to fit after it's pressed.

3. Sew 32 bright-colored batik 2" squares together end to end. Press the seam allowances open. Make two border units.

4. Sew border units to the long sides. The units should fit perfectly. Press the seam allowances toward the border.

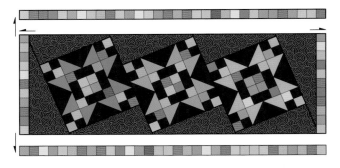

Finishing the Table Runner

1. Prepare the runner backing and batting. Layer and baste the backing, batting, and quilt top.

2. Quilt as inspired. The table runner shown was finished with a medium-scale design I call Swoosh and Swirl. This scale allows the runner to remain soft and gives it a nice texture. I chose a turquoise thread to contrast with the colors of the quilt. The turquoise is bright enough to be seen on both the black and colored batiks.

3. Prepare and attach the binding and label. Refer to "Binding Your Quilt" on page 76 if you need help with this step.

RING OF FIRE

Pieced and quilted by Sheila Sinclair Snyder

Finished quilt: 48½" x 60½"

Finished blocks: 6" x 6"

Materials

Yardage amounts are based on 42"-wide fabric.

1⅓ yards *total* of assorted bright plaids and striped fabrics for blocks

1⅛ yards of black plaid for blocks and background squares

1⅛ yards of dark blue plaid for blocks and background squares

½ yard of fabric for binding

3 yards of fabric for backing

55" x 67" piece of batting

Cutting

All cutting instructions include ¼"-wide seam allowances.

From the assorted bright plaids and striped fabrics, cut:

30 squares, 6⅞" x 6⅞"; cut each square in half diagonally to make 60 triangles

From the black plaid, cut:

1 strip, 6⅞" x 42"; crosscut into 5 squares, 6⅞" x 6⅞". Cut each square in half diagonally to make 10 triangles

4 strips, 6½" x 42"; crosscut into 20 squares, 6½" x 6½"

From the dark blue plaid, cut

1 strip, 6⅞" x 42"; crosscut into 5 squares, 6⅞" x 6⅞". Cut each square in half diagonally to make 10 triangles

4 strips, 6½" x 6½"; crosscut into 20 squares, 6½" x 6½"

From the binding fabric, cut:

6 strips, 2" x 42"

Making the Blocks

1. Using a design wall, lay out all of the triangles before piecing. Refer to the quilt diagram on page 23 or to the photo on page 22. Handle the diagonal edges of the triangles carefully to avoid stretching and distortion. Arrange and rearrange the units for the best color combinations. Add the black and dark blue plaid background squares, alternating colors to create a checkerboard look.

2. Sew the bright triangles together to make half-square-triangle units. Press the seam allowances open. Make 20, replacing the half-square-triangle units on the design wall as you go. Repeat to make 10 of a bright triangle combined with a dark blue plaid and 10 of a bright triangle combined with a black plaid. Press the seam allowances toward the dark fabric. Replace each square on the design wall as you go.

Make 20.

Make 10.   Make 10.

Doesn't everyone love plaids and stripes together?! Here's your opportunity to make your own "Ring of Fire" with high contrast for a high-power graphic effect. There's nothing that's country style about my quilt or the colors I used, but if you like that look, it would be fabulous in earthy colors as well. Use regular woven quilting cotton, homespun, or flannel—your choice!

A BIT ABOUT THE BORDER

Unlike a traditional straight border, the color placement of the dark squares and triangles are used to mimic the look of a medallion block set on-point. But really, the entire quilt consists of simple squares or half-square triangle blocks sewn together in straight rows for a very easy, yet dramatic quilt.

Assembling the Quilt Top

1. You should now have 10 rows of eight blocks each on your design wall. Make sure that the dark blue and the black plaid background squares create the checkerboard effect.

2. Sew the blocks together into rows. Press the seam allowances in opposite directions from row to row. Sew the rows together; press.

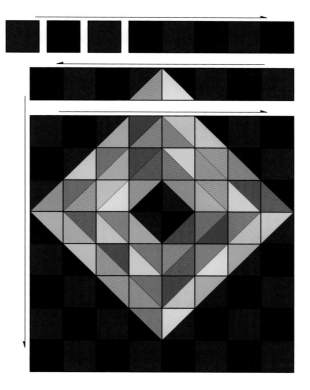

Finishing the Quilt

1. Piece the quilt backing using a horizontal seam. Layer and baste the backing, batting, and quilt top.

2. Quilt as inspired. The quilt shown was finished with an echoed flame motif in red around the edge of the quilt. There is a similar-shaped flower motif overlapping both edges of the bright-colored center diamond. The dark background of the quilt was finished with royal blue thread in one of my favorite designs called Swoosh and Swirl, and this was used in the bright-colored center in a smaller scale with gold thread. It was such a fun and fast quilt to work on I was disappointed when it was finished!

3. Prepare and attach the binding and label. Refer to "Binding Your Quilt" on page 76 if you need help with this step.

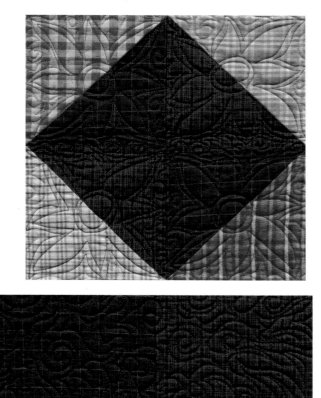

Swiss Army Quilt

Pieced and quilted by Sheila Sinclair Snyder

Finished quilt: 72½" x 90½"

Finished blocks: 9" x 9", 4½" x 9", and 4½" x 4½"

Materials

Yardage amounts are based on 42"-wide fabric.

3¼ yards of light print for blocks*

2⅞ yards of red solid for blocks

1 yard of white fabric for blocks

⅜ yard of black print for blocks

⅔ yard of fabric for binding

6 yards of fabric for backing

78" x 96" piece of batting

* You can use a directional print as I did; the instructions are written to accommodate a directional print.

Cutting

All cutting instructions include ¼"-wide seam allowances.

From the red solid, cut:
16 strips, 4½" x 42"
8 strips, 2½" x 42"

From the white fabric, cut:
10 strips, 1½" x 42"; crosscut *2* of the strips into
    14 rectangles, 1½" x 5"
8 strips, 1½" x 42"; crosscut into 32 rectangles,
    1½" x 9½"
5 strips, 1" x 42"; crosscut *1* strip into 4 rectangles,
    1" x 5"

From the black print, cut:
7 strips, 1½" x 42"; crosscut into:
    124 squares, 1½" x 1½"
    72 rectangles, 1" x 1½"

From the light print, cut:
10 strips, 9½" x 42"; crosscut into:
    31 squares, 9½" x 9½"
    10 rectangles, 5" x 9½"
2 strips, 5" x 42"; crosscut into 8 rectangles, 5" x 9½"
    (cutting in this direction allows for the directional print to flow in the same direction)

From the binding fabric, cut:
8 strips, 2" x 42"

Making the Blocks

You'll make two different blocks for this quilt: the Swiss Army block in three different sizes and an alternate block in two different sizes.

Swiss Army Center Blocks

1. Sew a red 4½"-wide strip to each long edge of a white 1½"-wide strip. Press the seam allowances toward the red fabric. Make eight strip sets. Crosscut the strip sets into 64 rectangles 4½" x 9½".

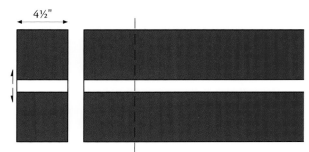

Make 8 strip sets.
Cut 64 segments.

24

The emblem on the Swiss army knife caught my eye as I was paging through a catalog, and I realized it could be put into a quilt design that would be very graphic and masculine. This generous twin-size quilt would be just right for a college student.

2. Sew red/white/red segments to both sides of a white 1½" x 9½" strip. Press the seam allowances toward the red fabric. Make 32 blocks.

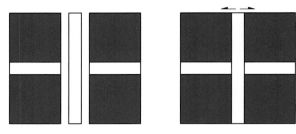

Make 32.

Swiss Army Corner Blocks

1. Sew a red 2½"-wide strip to each long side of a white 1"-wide strip. Press the seam allowances toward the red fabric. Make four strip sets. Crosscut one strip set into eight segments, 2½" x 5". Set the remaining strip sets aside.

Make 4 strip sets.
Cut one strip set into 8 segments.

2. Sew a red/white/red segment to each long side of a white 1" x 5" strip. Press the seam allowances toward the red fabric. Make four blocks.

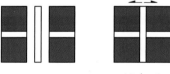

Make 4.

Swiss Army Border Blocks

1. Using the remaining strip sets from the corner blocks, cut 28 segments, 4½" x 5".

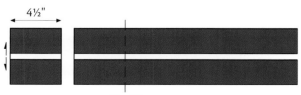

Cut 28 segments.

2. Sew a red/white/red segment to each long side of a white 1½" x 5" rectangle. Press the seam allowances toward the red fabric. Make 14 blocks.

Make 14.

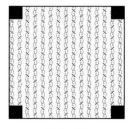

A BIT ABOUT THE BORDER

At first glance, this quilt doesn't even seem to have a border. Look closer and you'll see that rectangular blocks that are half the width of the center blocks encircle this quilt, adding the finishing touch to this graphic design. The border corner blocks are square, smaller versions of the blocks in the center of the quilt.

Alternate Center Blocks

1. Finger-press a ¼" seam allowance on two adjacent edges of a black 1½" square.

2. Place the square on the corner of a light print 9½" square, aligning the raw edges. Appliqué in place. Repeat for the remaining three corners of the block. Press from the wrong side. Trim the background from under the appliqué to ¼". Make 31 blocks.

Make 31.

Alternate Border Blocks

1. Finger-press a ¼" seam allowance on two adjacent edges of a black 1" x 1½" rectangle.

2. Place the rectangle on the corner of a light print 5" x 9½" rectangle, aligning the raw edges. Appliqué in place. Repeat for the remaining three corners of the block. Press from the wrong side. Trim the background from under the appliqué to ¼". Make a total of 18 blocks as shown.

Make 10.   Make 8.

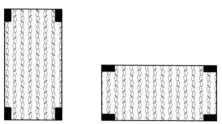

designer's tip:
MINIMIZE SEAMS

Appliquéing the black cornerstones to the alternate blocks allows you to use a directional print for the background without having any seams that would break up the print.

Assembling the Quilt

1. Arrange the blocks in rows, referring to the quilt diagram for guidance. Take care to place each alternate block so the direction of the print is consistent.

2. Sew the blocks into rows. Press the seam allowances toward the red blocks.

3. Sew the rows together. Press the seam allowances all in one direction.

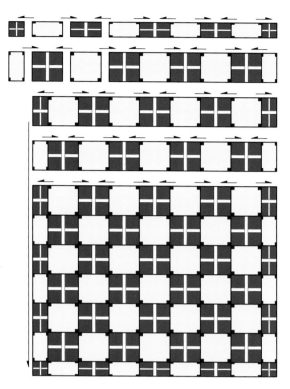

Finishing the Quilt

1. Piece the quilt backing using a vertical seam. Layer and baste the backing, batting, and quilt top.

2. Quilt as inspired. The quilt shown was finished with a large-scale design I call Curls. This scale allows the quilt to remain soft and gives it a nice texture. I chose rich wheat-colored thread to contrast with the colors of the quilt and be strong enough to be seen on all the fabrics.

3. Prepare and attach the binding and label. Refer to "Binding Your Quilt" on page 76 if you need help with this step.

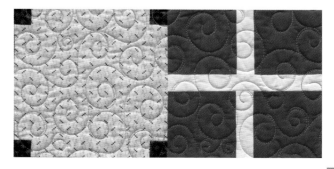

SHOOTING STARS

Pieced by Sheila Sinclair Snyder; quilted by Lisa Bee Wilson

Finished quilt: 85½" x 97"

Finished blocks: 9" x 9"

Finished border blocks: 6½" x 9"

Materials

Yardage amounts are based on 42"-wide fabric.

7¼ yards of print for background

1 yard *each* of five different coordinating prints for the stars and inner border

¾ yard of fabric for binding

8 yards of fabric for backing

92" x 103" piece of batting

Cutting

All cutting instructions include ¼"-wide seam allowances.

From *each* of the five different coordinating prints, cut:

4 strips, 5½" x 42"; crosscut into 64 rectangles, 2½" x 5½"

2 strips, 2½" x 42", crosscut into 6 rectangles, 2½" x 9½"

From *each of two* of the coordinating prints, cut:

1 square, 2½" x 2½"

From the background print, cut:

10 strips, 8" x 42"; crosscut into 160 rectangles, 2½" x 8"

16 strips, 7⅛" x 42"; crosscut into 80 squares, 7⅛" x 7⅛". Cut each square in half diagonally to make 160 triangles

7 strips, 5" x 42"; crosscut into 28 rectangles, 5" x 9½"

1 strip, 5" x 42"; crosscut into:
2 rectangles 5" x 7"
2 rectangles, 2½" x 5"

From the binding fabric, cut:

10 strips, 2" x 42"

designer's tip: STAY ORGANIZED

The stars in this quilt sweep across the quilt in diagonal rows of color. Staying organized while making this quilt is essential. Here's what I did.

1. Decide on a color sequence and label each of your five coordinating prints with a letter, A–E. Note that A and E will create the longest diagonal rows of stars that are more or less in the center of the quilt.

2. On a piece of paper, create a chart similar to the one below.

3. Cut four small snippets from each of the five fabrics. Glue or tape the snippets to the chart in each position. Now you can rely on the chart to help you stay organized.

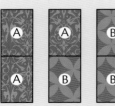
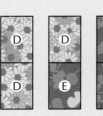

I originally designed this quilt as a wedding gift a few years back, and of course I gave it away. Finding this colorful print inspired me to make it again. Choosing the coordinating star fabrics was easy with such a fabulous background fabric to work with. Start the hunt now for your own collection!

Making the Hunter's Star Blocks

The Hunter's Star is a simple approach to piecing a complex eight-pointed star.

1. To make a base unit, pin a 2½" x 5½" rectangle of fabric A to each end of a 2½" x 8" background rectangle with right sides together as shown. Draw a diagonal line from corner to corner and sew on the marked line.

2. Trim away the excess fabric at the corners, leaving a ¼" seam allowance. Press the seam allowances as shown. As you press each base unit, fold the unit in half and use the tip of the iron to press a small crease at the midpoint as shown.

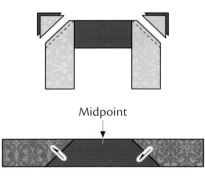

Midpoint

3. Finger-press the midpoint of the long side of a background print triangle.

Midpoint

4. With right sides together, match the midpoints of the base unit and the background triangle. Note the base unit will be longer than the triangle. Sew the units together. Press the seam allowances toward the base unit.

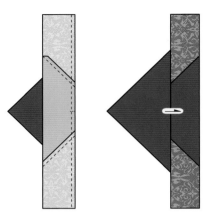

5. Repeat steps 1–4 to make a second pieced triangle.

6. Sew the pieced triangles together as shown. Press the seam allowances open. Trim and square up the block to 9½" x 9½".

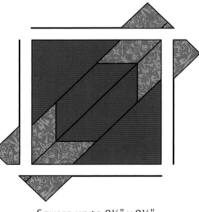

Square up to 9½" x 9½".

7. Repeat steps 1–6 to make a total of eight blocks with fabric A on both ends.

8. Pin a 2½" x 5½" rectangle of fabric A to one end of a 2½" x 8½" background rectangle and a 2½" x 5½" rectangle of fabric B to the other end. Make eight base units in this manner and eight with fabric A and B on opposite sides of the background rectangle. Press the seam allowances as you did in step 2. When joined together, fabrics A and B will match on each end.

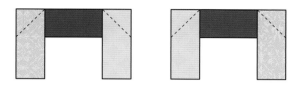

Make 8.

Make 8.

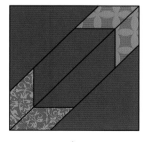

Make 8.

9. Referring to the chart, repeat the steps for each color combination. You'll make 16 base units of each color combination, which will make eight blocks each. As you finish each color combination, keep those blocks together and the whole series in sequence. This will allow for quicker and easier layout of the quilt.

Making the Border and Corner Blocks

1. Sew a 5" x 9½" background rectangle to a 2½" x 9½" coordinating rectangle. Do not press yet; this will be done in a later step. Make 28 border blocks. There will be two extra coordinating fabric rectangles that will not be used.

Make 28.

2. Sew a 2½" coordinating square to a 2½" x 5" background rectangle. Press the seam allowances open. Make two units.

Make 2.

3. Lay out the units from step 2 with a 5" x 7" background rectangle as shown. Sew the units together. Make two corner blocks. Do not press at this time.

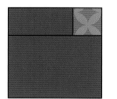 

Lower-left
corner of quilt

Lower-right
corner of quilt

A BIT ABOUT THE BORDER

While it looks as if a light narrow inner pieced border cuts right through some of the Hunter's Star blocks, the narrow border is actually part of the border blocks. Both the inner and outer border fabrics make up the outer-border pieced blocks, pieced right along with the center blocks. It's hard to tell the outer border is pieced, because the print is busy, and the same print is used for the entire outer border. Amazingly deceptive—and effective!

Assembling the Quilt Top

1. Arrange the Hunter's Star blocks in 10 rows of eight blocks each. Carefully place the color combinations in order to achieve the diagonal rows of each colored star.

2. Add the border blocks to the sides and bottom of the quilt. Add the corner blocks at the bottom of the quilt. Arrange the colors and prints to the best effect.

3. Remove the border blocks from the arrangement and press the seam allowances so that they're pressed in opposite directions from block to block. Replace the blocks in the layout.

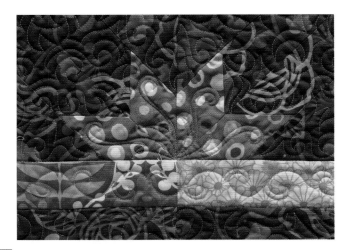

4. Sew the blocks into rows. Press the seam allowances in opposite directions from row to row. Sew the rows together and press.

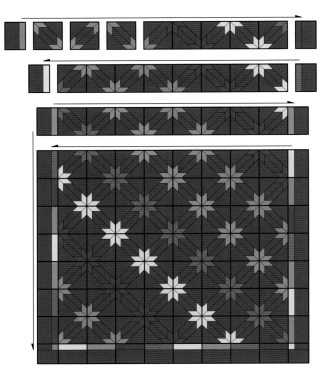

Finishing the Quilt

1. Piece the quilt backing using two horizontal seams. Layer and baste the backing, batting, and quilt top.

2. Quilt as inspired. Lisa and I brainstormed the quilting plan for this quilt. I'd seen another quilt she'd previously done with a fun motif in a star and (my favorite) Swoosh and Swirl in a medium scale in the background. We decided to use mustard-colored thread, which suits both the background and the stars.

3. Prepare and attach the binding and label. Refer to "Binding Your Quilt" on page 76 if you need help with this step.

SPINAL CORD

Pieced by Sheila Sinclair Snyder; quilted by Lisa Bee Wilson

Finished quilt: 90½" x 102½"

Finished blocks: Irregular, 12" x 12" at the widest point

Materials

Yardage amounts are based on 42"-wide fabrics.

3½ yards of black solid for blocks

3½ yards of gray solid for blocks

3½ yards *total* of assorted solids for sashing and borders

⅞ yard of fabric for binding

8⅛ yards of fabric for backing

96" x 108" piece of batting

Template plastic

designer's tip:
ADD VARIETY

You may choose, as I did, to replace a few of the 3½"-wide strips with a pieced unit. I sewed together three 1½"-wide strips, pressed the seam allowances open, and used this constructed strip as if it were a solid piece. Keep that in mind as you cut the assorted solid-colored fabrics.

Cutting

All cutting instructions include ¼"-wide seam allowances.

From the assorted solids, cut:

24 strips, 3½" x 42"

8 rectangles, 4" x 12½"

From the black solid, cut:

9 strips, 12½" x 42"; crosscut into 36 rectangles, 9" x 12½"

From the gray solid, cut:

9 strips, 12½" x 42"; crosscut into 36 rectangles, 9" x 12½"

From the binding fabric, cut:

10 strips, 2" x 42"

Making the Strip Sets

If you wish to sew together narrow strips to replace a 3½"-wide solid strip, do so now. Press the seam allowances open and use spray sizing while you're pressing to help keep the unit straight and the seam allowances under control. Use these constructed strips randomly in the strip-set construction that follows.

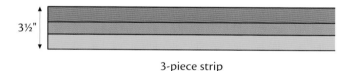

3½" ↕

3-piece strip

1. Sew two 3½"-wide assorted solid strips together along one long edge. Press the seam allowances open. Add a third and fourth strip, pressing the seam allowances open as you go. Make six strip sets.

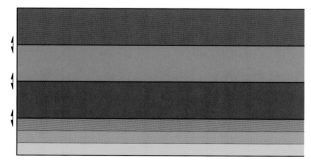

Make 6 strip sets.

The first view of this graphic quilt looks like rows of divided rectangles separated by rows of bright, pieced sashing. So, I think you'll be surprised by the construction of the block, and then the name will make sense! Working with solid fabrics was fun and allowed for some interesting effects that wouldn't have been as graphic with prints.

2. Crosscut each strip set into five or six segments, 3½" wide, and then cut the remainder of the strip set into 1½"-wide segments. This will give you the best color variety. You'll need a total of 31 segments, 3½" wide, and 72 segments, 1½" wide. Separate one of the 3½"-wide segments into two units of two squares each.

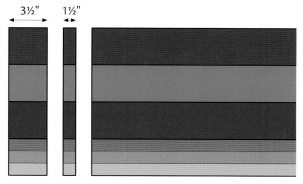

Cut 31 segments, 3½" wide,
and 72 segments, 1½" wide.

Making the Spinal Cord Blocks

1. Use the pattern on pages 38 and 39 and template plastic to make template A.

2. Place template A on a 9" x 12½" black rectangle. Draw a line along the diagonal edge, and then cut with a ruler and rotary cutter to make two black pieces. Cut all of the black rectangles in this manner.

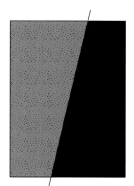

Cut using template A.

3. Repeat step 2 using template A on the 9" x 12½" gray rectangles.

4. Arrange one black piece A, one 1½"-wide colored segment and one gray piece A to make one Spinal Cord block as shown. Sew the block together. Do not press at this time. Make 40 blocks with the black piece on the left side of the block. Make 32 blocks with the gray piece on the left.

Make 40.

Make 32.

Prepare the Setting Triangles

1. Use the pattern on pages 38 and 39 to make template B using template plastic.

2. Place template B on a 4" x 12½" assorted solid rectangle. Draw a line along the edge of the template; then cut the piece along the drawn line using a ruler and rotary cutter. Repeat for

all 8 rectangles. *Note:* If using a print that has a right and wrong side, cut 4 and 4 reversed.

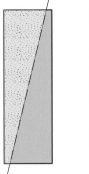

Cut 4 using template B.

Cut 4 using template B reversed.

A BIT ABOUT THE BORDER

The outer pieced borders on this quilt look similar, yet the sides are joined a little bit differently from the top and bottom. The side border is made of units the same height as the blocks. They're joined to the sides of the quilt at the same time the rows are sewn together, so you can just treat them like any other block in the row. The top and bottom borders are each sewn together as one long border strip before being joined to the quilt. But don't worry if they don't quite fit. With all the small bits of color in this quilt, if you end up needing to trim one of the colored squares to be a bit narrower, no one will give it a second thought.

Assembling the Quilt Top

1. Arrange the blocks in eight rows of nine blocks each, referring to the quilt diagram on page 37 for guidance. Shuffle the Spinal Cord blocks as needed for the best placement of the scrappy-colored segments.

2. Place a setting triangle at the beginning and end of each row of blocks.

3. Place a 3½"-wide colored segment at the beginning and end of each row of blocks.

4. Place seven colored segments and one two-piece unit at the top edge of the quilt. Repeat for the bottom edge.

5. Rearrange any blocks, setting triangles, or border elements to get a good distribution of colors.

6. Sew the top border into a row; press the seam allowances open. Repeat for the bottom border.

7. To sew the blocks in row one, mark the top edge of the first block with the row number. Sew the setting triangles to the adjoining Spinal Cord block. Press the blocks in the following manner: For any block that faces "up" (with the wide edge of the block at the top), press the seam allowances toward the center. For any block that faces "down" (the wide edge of the block at the bottom), press the seam allowances away from the center. When joining the blocks, *always* press the seam allowances *toward* the black fabric and *away* from the gray fabric.

designer's tip: SEWING ODD-SHAPED UNITS

Before you sew the first two angled units together, draw the ¼" seam allowances onto the fabric using a sharp pencil or chalk. Match and pin the seam allowances at each end; then add pins in between to keep the pieces from slipping. The pieces will be offset at each end. Stitch the seam. Press the seam allowances as noted in the instructions and check for accuracy. Use this unit as a sample for making all the units.

8. Sew a border unit to each end of the row. Press the seam allowances toward the setting triangle. Repeat this pressing for all odd-numbered rows.

Pressing for odd rows

9. Repeat step 7 to sew the blocks and setting triangles in row two. Be sure to mark the top edge of the first block with the row number.

10. Sew a border unit to each end of the row. Press the seam allowances toward the border. Repeat this pressing for all even-numbered rows.

Pressing for even rows

11. Continue sewing blocks into rows. Sew the rows together, including the top and bottom borders; press.

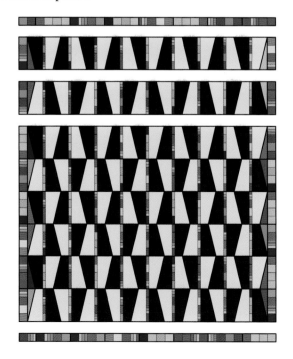

Finishing the Quilt

1. Piece the quilt backing using two horizontal seams. Layer and baste the backing, batting, and quilt top.

2. Quilt as inspired. Lisa and I brainstormed the quilting plan for this quilt. Together we came up with a plan that neither of us would have thought of on our own. We decided on a combination of large-scale curls with tails alternated with a graphic border and background quilting. Then the fun of choosing the thread color began! We used a fabulous variegated thread for the larger motifs and a variety of solid colors for the background. Didn't Lisa do an awesome job quilting?

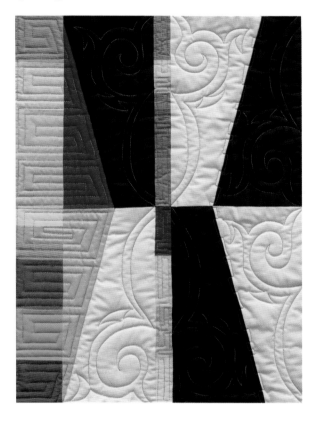

3. Prepare and attach the binding and label. Refer to "Binding Your Quilt" on page 76 if you need help with this step.

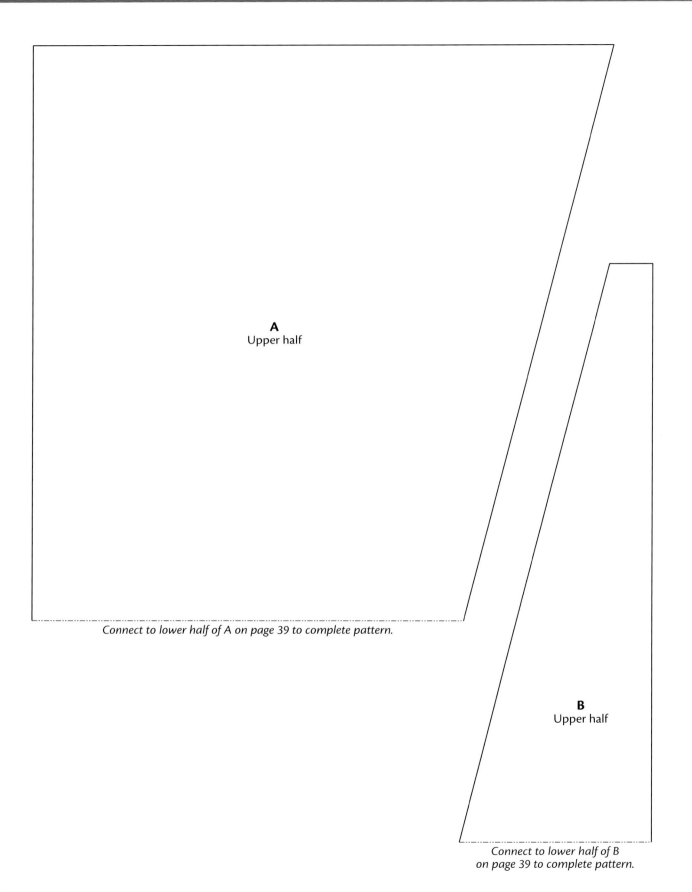

A
Upper half

Connect to lower half of A on page 39 to complete pattern.

B
Upper half

*Connect to lower half of B
on page 39 to complete pattern.*

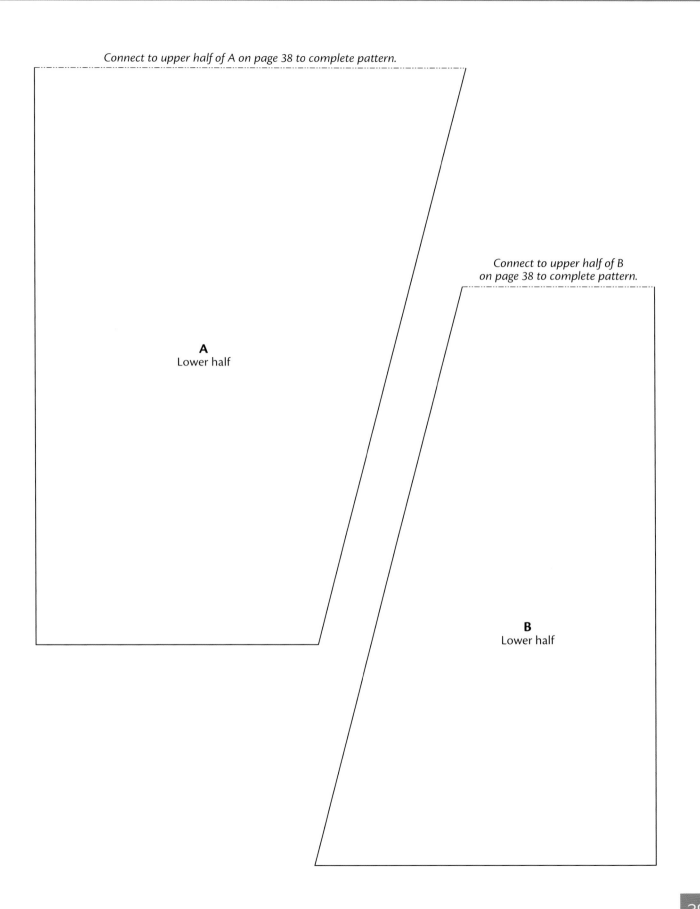

Connect to upper half of A on page 38 to complete pattern.

Connect to upper half of B
on page 38 to complete pattern.

A
Lower half

B
Lower half

STARGAZING

Pieced, appliquéd, and quilted by Sheila Sinclair Snyder

Finished quilt: 38" x 45½"

Finished border blocks: 7½" x 7½"

Materials

Yardage amounts are based on 42"-wide fabric.

1⅔ yards *total* of assorted coordinating and accent fabrics for the border blocks

⅔ yard of dark print for sky background

⅓ yard *or* 1 fat quarter of light print for house

¼ yard of dark large-scale floral for garden

¼ yard of bright print for inner border

Assorted scraps for the house appliqués, including a striped fabric for the steps

½ yard *each* of two different 2"-wide velvet ribbons for the big and little dippers

⅛ yard of close-weave organza

⅛ yard of loose-weave netting

½ yard of fabric for binding

2½ yards fabric for backing

44" x 51" piece of batting

Freezer paper for templates

Assorted embellishments and charms of your choice*

* *I added Dimensions wool-felt embellishment flowers purchased at my local quilt shop, a metallic star, and a button for the doorknob.*

Cutting

All cutting instructions include ¼"-wide seam allowances.

From the dark print, cut:
1 rectangle, 21" x 28½"

From the dark large-scale floral print, cut:
1 rectangle, 7" x 21"

From the bright print, cut:
4 strips, 1¾" x 42"; crosscut into:
    2 strips, 1¾" x 28"
    2 strips, 1¾" x 23"

From the assorted coordinating and accent fabrics, cut:
30 to 35 strips of varied widths from 1" x 42" up to 3" x 42"

From several of the darkest coordinating and accent fabrics, cut:
18 squares, 2½" x 2½"

From the binding fabric, cut:
5 strips, 2" x 42"

The Milky Way, the Big Dipper, and Little Dipper seem to fill the night sky and light up the castle in this dreamland. Find a large-scale floral on black for the patch of flower garden that the castle sits on. This fun appliquéd and pieced project was inspired by my friend Tonye Belinda Phillips, a wonderful appliqué artist. Be sure to check out her website (www.tonyebelindaphillips.com) and see for yourself why she and her work are so inspiring.

Appliquéing the Center

Follow the instructions on page 75 in "Needle-Turn Appliqué" or use your favorite method of appliqué. Reverse the patterns if you use fusible web.

1. Use the patterns on pages 45–48 to make a template out of freezer paper for each piece of the appliqué. Trace all of the templates for the house onto the fabric of your choice. Cut out the appliqués, adding the necessary seam allowance.

2. Cut a gentle curve in the large-scale print, referring to the photograph on page 41 for guidance. Position it on the background.

3. Position and pin the house with door, step, sidewalk, windows, staircase, roof, and chimney onto the background.

4. Appliqué the designs in place. I started with the chimney, and then worked down, layering each piece as needed.

designer's tip:
GO WITH THE PRINT

The fabric I chose for the door frame had a print that resembled stones, so I used that to my advantage and cut following the print. Use a similar fabric for the same effect, or go with the pattern provided on page 48 to create the effect of a wooden door frame.

5. Using the templates for the Milky Way, cut the shapes from organza and netting, without adding a seam allowance. Appliqué these in place using a running stitch ⅛" from the raw edges of each piece. I used a silver metallic thread to give it a nice sparkle. Embellish with more running stitches throughout the Milky Way if desired.

6. Cut seven large circles from one velvet ribbon for the Big Dipper and six small circles from the other ribbon for the Little Dipper, adding a seam allowance when cutting. I cut one large circle for the North Star in the Little Dipper. Appliqué in place.

7. Trim the appliqué block to 20½" x 28".

Making the Half Log Cabin Blocks

The blocks are constructed with improvisational piecing; strips are cut at the machine as you sew. This allows for a very scrappy effect and an opportunity to use strips that are not quite perfect or straight. Set up a small ironing surface and cutting board close to your sewing machine to make the cutting and sewing of these blocks as efficient as possible. Varying the width of the strips within blocks will make them more interesting and exciting in the finished project.

1. Pick up a dark 2½" square and one of the assorted strips. Use the square to estimate the length needed and cut this length from the strip with a rotary cutter or scissors. It's best to cut it a little longer than needed.

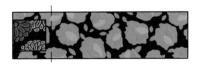

2. Sew the two pieces together. Press the seam allowances toward the newly added piece. This will be the case for each strip you add. Trim the edges even with the first piece.

3. Pick up a second assorted strip. This will be added to the end of the seam you just sewed. Estimate the length of strip needed as before, cut and sew in place. Press and trim.

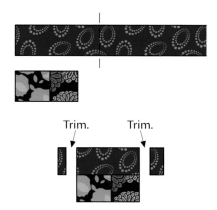

Trim.   Trim.

4. Repeat this process to add a third strip, adding one strip at a time and alternating sides. Always keep the first square in one corner of the block. Keep adding strips until your block is about 9" square. I used anywhere from 10 to 13 strips, depending on the widths.

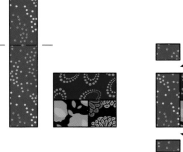

←Trim.

←Trim.

5. Square up the finished block to exactly 8" x 8". I angled the ruler when trimming, to create some interesting angles in the final block.

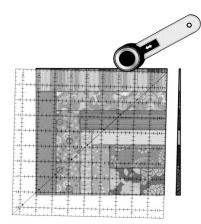

Make 18.

6. Repeat to make 18 blocks.

A BIT ABOUT THE BORDER

What a fun, randomly pieced border! Looks challenging to fit, doesn't it? The secret is to trim the appliqué centerpiece to the dimensions given, add the plain inner border, and then trim up those wonky blocks all to the same specified size. Because the strips in these blocks are random width and sometimes skewed, trimming the finished blocks and lopping off what's not needed just adds more character!

Assembling the Quilt Top

1. Sew the 1¾" x 28" inner-border strips to the sides of the appliqué block. Press the seam allowances toward the border. Sew the 1¾" x 23" strips to the top and bottom of the appliquéd block. Press the seam allowances toward the border.

2. Arrange the border Half Log Cabin blocks around the appliquéd center. Rearrange as needed for a pleasing effect.

3. Sew the five top blocks together into a row. Press the seam allowances of the two end blocks toward the middle, and the other seam allowances toward one side. Repeat for the bottom row.

4. Sew four side border blocks together. Press the seam allowances in one direction. Position and pin in place at the side of the appliqué center. Sew the seam; press the seam allowances toward the outer blocks. Repeat for the second side border.

5. Position and pin the top border on the appliqué center. Sew the seam; press the seam allowances toward the outside. Repeat for the bottom border.

Finishing the Quilt

1. Piece the quilt backing using a horizontal seam. Layer, and then baste the backing, batting, and quilt top.

2. Quilt as inspired. The quilt shown was so much fun to quilt, with wavy lines in the sky, details on the castle, flowers in the garden, and funky stars with circles in the borders. Using both variegated and solid-colored thread added to the whimsy of this quilt.

3. After the project was quilted, I added a few more embellishments, including the button doorknob and felted wool flowers.

4. Prepare and attach the binding and label. Refer to "Binding Your Quilt" on page 76 if you need help with this step.

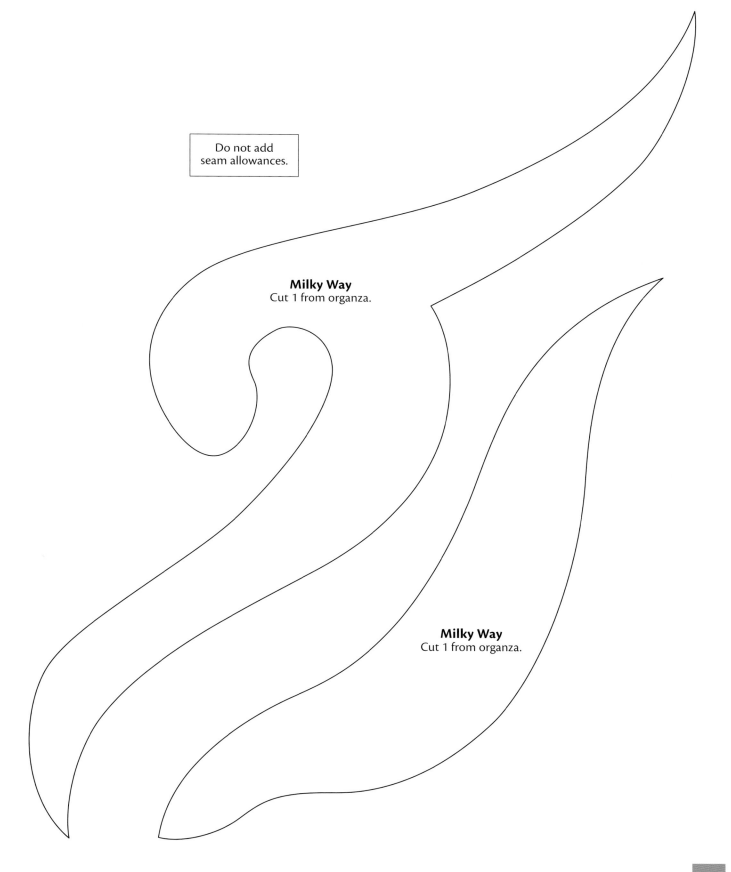

Do not add
seam allowances.

Milky Way
Cut 1 from organza.

Milky Way
Cut 1 from organza.

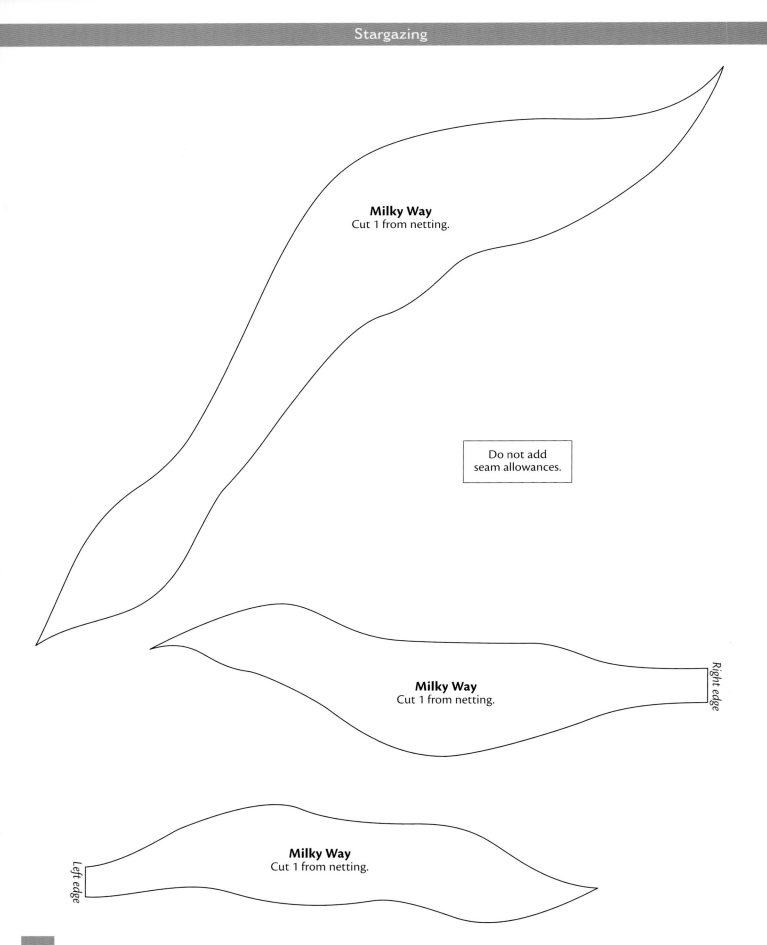

Milky Way
Cut 1 from netting.

Do not add
seam allowances.

Milky Way
Cut 1 from netting.

Right edge

Milky Way
Cut 1 from netting.

Left edge

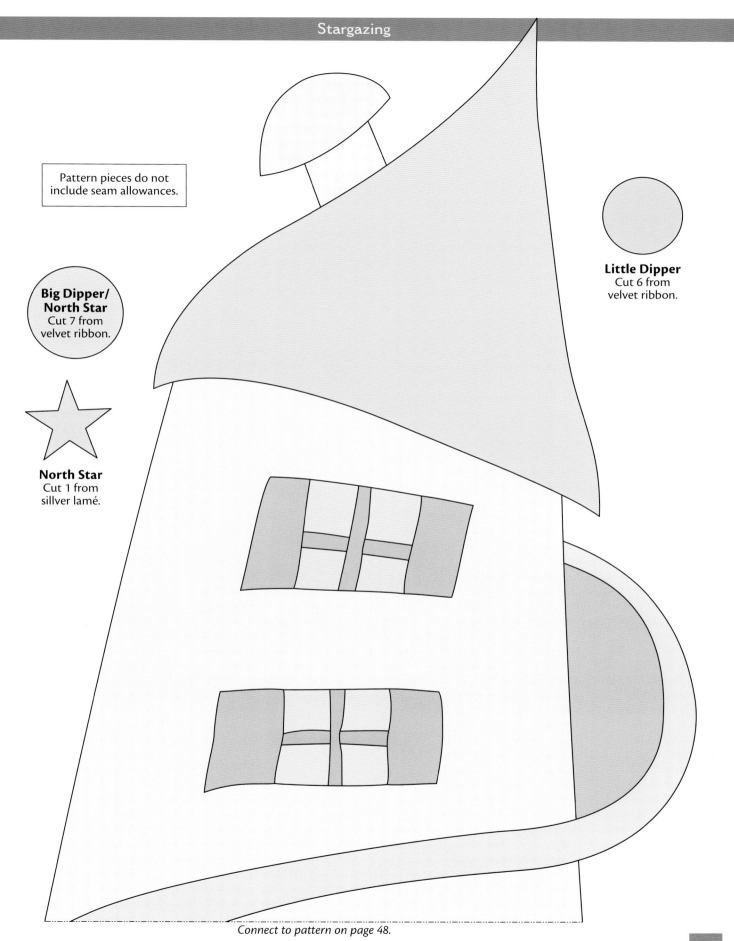

Pattern pieces do not include seam allowances.

Big Dipper/ North Star Cut 7 from velvet ribbon.

North Star Cut 1 from sillver lamé.

Little Dipper Cut 6 from velvet ribbon.

Connect to pattern on page 48.

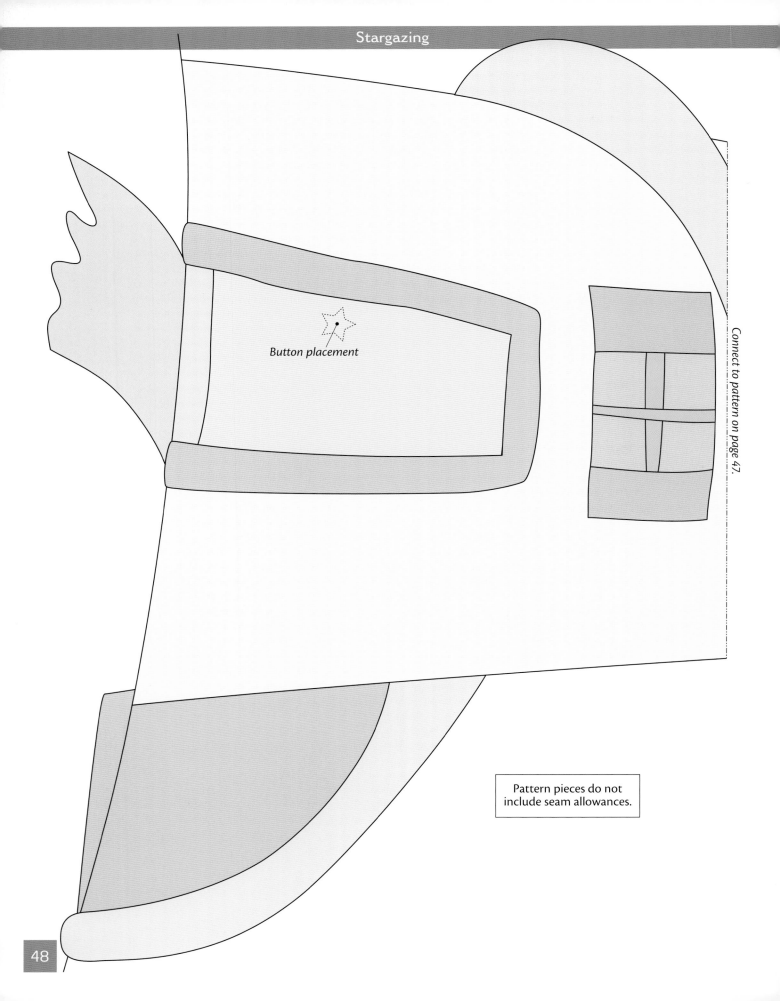

Button placement

Connect to pattern on page 47.

Pattern pieces do not
include seam allowances.

CONVERSATION STARTER

Pieced by Penny Hutchens, Cynthia Brunz, Lisa Bee Wilson, and Sheila Sinclair Snyder;
appliquéd and quilted by Sheila Sinclair Snyder

Finished quilt: 56½" x 56½"

Finished border blocks: 8" x 8"

Materials

Yardage amounts are based on 42"-wide fabric.

1⅜ yards of bright print for appliqué and border blocks

⅞ yard of dark print for appliqué background and border blocks

⅞ yard *total* of assorted florals for border blocks

⅞ yard *total* of assorted solids for pieced borders

½ yard of floral print 1 for outer border

⅜ yard of floral print 2 for inner border

¼ yard of solid for cornerstones

½ yard of fabric for binding

3½ yards of fabric for backing

62" x 62" piece of batting

Freezer paper for the template

Cutting

All cutting instructions include ¼"-wide seam allowances.

From the dark print, cut:
1 square, 25" x 25"

From the bright print, cut:
1 square, 25" x 25"
4 strips, 4⅞" x 42", crosscut into 32 squares, 4⅞" x 4⅞"; cut the squares in half diagonally to make 64 triangles

From the solid for cornerstones, cut:
2 strips, 2½" x 42", crosscut into 32 squares, 2½" x 2½"

From the assorted solids, cut:
144 squares, 2½" x 2½"

From the floral print 2 for inner border, cut:
4 strips, 2½" x 42", crosscut into 4 strips, 2½" x 28½"

From *1* of the assorted florals, cut:
1 strip, 4½" x 42", crosscut into 8 squares, 4½" x 4½"

From the remainder of assorted florals and the appliqué background fabric, cut:
16 squares, 2½" x 2½"
16 squares*, 6³⁄₁₆" x 6³⁄₁₆"

From the floral print 1 for outer border, cut:
6 strips, 2½" x 42"

From the binding fabric, cut:
6 strips, 2" x 42"

* To cut 6³⁄₁₆" squares, cut halfway between the 6⅛" line and the 6¼" line on your ruler.

Appliquéing the Center Block

Follow the instructions on page 75 in "Needle-Turn Appliqué" or use your favorite method of appliqué.

1. Use the pattern on page 54 and freezer paper to make a template for the appliqué. You can trace the template in quarters or two halves if your freezer paper isn't large enough; add extra along the edges to overlap the pattern. Position the paper template onto your fabric and press in place. Trace the template onto the bright print and roughly cut out the appliqué, adding a generous turn-under allowance.

A round-robin challenge allowed me to use this Hawaiian appliqué as a centerpiece. I designed the appliqué motif a few years back and published it in my first book, *Pieced to Fit*, as a 12" block. Using it in a 24" scale made it much more dramatic, not to mention *easy* to appliqué! Passing it to my friends, who did more with it than I would have myself, was fun. It was such a surprise each month to see it evolving. Thanks to Penny, Cynthia, and Lisa for the original challenge, and for generously contributing to this quilt in such an artful way!

2. Center the appliqué fabric over the background fabric. Baste in place.

3. Appliqué the design to the background, trimming the seam allowance as you sew.

4. Press the block from the wrong side and trim to exactly 24½" x 24½".

Making the Square-in-a-Square Blocks

1. Choose one of the floral 6³⁄₁₆" squares. Center bright triangles along two opposite edges. Sew, and press the seam allowances toward the triangles. Repeat on the remaining two edges of the block. The block should measure 8½" x 8½". Make 16 blocks.

Make 16.

2. Sew four blocks into a row. Press the seam allowances in one direction. Make four rows. Each row should measure 8½" x 32½".

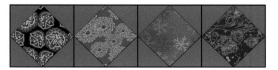

Make 4.

Making the Double Four-Patch Blocks

1. Sew a solid 2½" square of cornerstone fabric to a floral 2½" square. Press the seam allowances toward the solid fabric. Make 16 two-patch units.

Make 16.

2. Arrange and sew two units from step 1 together as shown to make a four-patch unit; press. Make eight.

Make 8.

3. Arrange and sew two four-patch units and two floral 4½" squares together as shown. Press the seam allowances toward the floral squares. The block should measure 8½" x 8½". Make four.

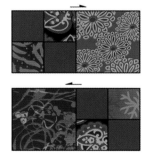 

Make 4.

A BIT ABOUT THE BORDER

Making an intricate pieced border—one with some blocks on point and others not—does require some careful planning and sewing. I find it easier to make the blocks that look on point first, as it's easier to fit the simpler patchwork to those than the other way around. For this project, of course, we've figured all the calculations for you. But I suggest that you sew with a scant ¼" seam allowance and measure all of the border blocks as you go to make sure they're the correct size. That way, when you sew the border blocks together, it will be easy to add them to the quilt and to other pieced border blocks.

Making the Pieced Border

1. Sew 12 of the assorted solid 2½" squares together into a row. Use a random pattern of color sequence. Press the seam allowances in one direction. Make four rows.

Make 4.

2. Repeat step 1 to sew 24 assorted solid 2½" squares together into a row. Make four rows.

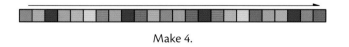

Make 4.

Cutting the Floral Outer Border

1. Piece the six floral 2½" x 42" border strips together into one long strip using diagonal seams. Trim the seam allowances to ¼". Press the seam allowances open. This will make a strip approximately 2½" x 240".

designer's tip: PRESSING ADVICE

Use spray sizing when pressing the long strip, to give it more stability as you finish the quilt.

2. Fold the strip in half lengthwise and in half again so you have four layers approximately 60" long.

3. Square up one end and make sure all the raw edges are aligned. Measure carefully from this edge and crosscut the strip at 52½".

52½"

Assembling the Quilt Top

1. Arrange the appliquéd center and first two borders, referring to the quilt diagram below. Sew the solid cornerstones to each end of the top and bottom pieced borders. Sew solid cornerstones to the top and bottom floral border strips. Press the seam allowances toward the borders.

2. Position and pin the pieced-squares border to opposite sides of the appliquéd center block. Sew and press the seam allowances toward the border. Press outward for each border that's added unless specified otherwise.

3. Position and pin the pieced-squares border with cornerstones to the top and bottom of the quilt center. Sew and press.

4. Position and pin the floral 2½" x 28½" borders to opposite sides of the quilt center. Sew and press. Repeat to add the floral 2½" x 28½" strip with cornerstones to the top and bottom.

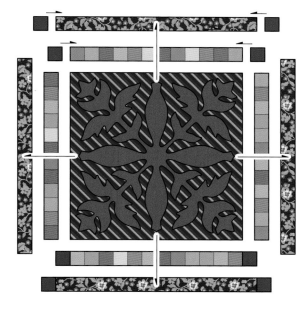

5. Position and pin a square-in-a-square border to opposite sides of the quilt. Sew and press inward.

6. Sew a Double Four-Patch block to each end of the remaining square-in-a-square borders and press toward the block. Position and pin these borders to the top and bottom of the quilt. Sew and press inward.

7. Repeat steps 2 and 3 to add the longer pieced-squares borders to each side of the project.

8. Sew floral 2½" x 52½" strips to opposite sides of the project and sew the remaining floral border with cornerstones to the top and bottom. Press.

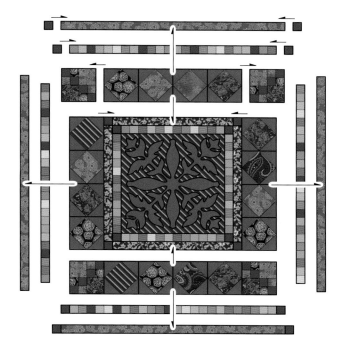

Finishing the Quilt

1. Piece the quilt backing using a vertical or horizontal seam. Layer and baste the backing, batting, and quilt top.

2. Quilt as inspired. This project was really exciting to quilt! Each border was treated separately with a trailing motif in the narrow borders and more flourish in the pieced blocks—all using the same variegated thread. The cornerstones seemed to march from the center to the outside edge, so they were quilted as a cohesive unit with a trailing flower. Since the appliqué has some larger elements, it needed some quilting too, and was done in a solid orange thread in swirls and spikes.

3. Prepare and attach the binding and label. Refer to "Binding Your Quilt" on page 76 if you need help with this step.

Flip pattern along this line.

Flip pattern along this line.

Center

Enlarge pattern 200%.
Pattern does not include
seam allowance.

WALLED GARDEN

Pieced and machine quilted by Sheila Sinclair Snyder
Finished quilt: 80½" x 96½"
Finished border blocks: 8" x 8"

Materials

Yardage amounts are based on 42"-wide fabric.

½ yard *each* of 20 assorted pink prints

4½ yards *total* of assorted dark green, brown, and burgundy prints

⅞ yard of fabric for binding

7½ yards of fabric for backing

86" x 102" piece of batting

Freezer paper

Cutting

All cutting instructions include ¼"-wide seam allowances.

From *each* of the 20 assorted pink prints, cut:
8 squares, 4½" x 4½"
2 strips, 2½" x 42"; crosscut into 20 squares, 2½" x 2½"
2 squares, 4⅞" x 4⅞"; cut the squares in half diagonally to make 4 triangles

From the variety of dark prints (green, brown, burgundy), cut:
400 squares, 2½" x 2½" (80 sets of 4 matching squares for center blocks and 40 sets of 2 matching squares for border blocks)
48 strips, 1½" x 42"

From the fabric for binding, cut:
9 strips, 2" x 42"

Making the Double Four-Patch Blocks

1. Sew two matching pink 2½" squares to two matching dark print 2½" squares as shown to make a four-patch unit. Make two.

Make 2.

2. Arrange two matching pink 4½" squares with the units from step 1, noting the placement of the brown squares. Sew the squares and four-patch units together in rows. Press the seam allowances toward the pink squares. Sew the two rows together to form a Double Four-Patch block; press the seam allowances to one side.

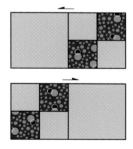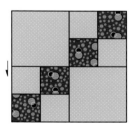

Make 80.

3. Repeat steps 1 and 2 to make a total of 80 Double Four-Patch blocks.

This quilt is essentially a pink and brown quilt with some green thrown in. This seems to be a perennially favorite color scheme. Whatever colors you choose, try using a mixture of fat quarters, fat eighths, and leftovers from other projects to make good use of your stash and achieve a really scrappy look.

A BIT ABOUT THE BORDER

I love the intricate look that this border gives to a quilt. First, it lets you finish the look of the diagonal patchwork chain by using a four-patch unit on one side of the blocks. Then the scrappy, strippy triangles on the other side of the blocks act as a darker zigzag frame around the whole quilt. Each border block is the same size as the blocks in the center, so when you're done sewing the rows together, the border is already attached.

Making the Border Blocks

The blocks used around the perimeter of the quilt are made from two pieced triangles. One triangle consists of a four-patch unit and two smaller triangles. The other, a Roman Stripe triangle, is made of strips. The border blocks are the same size as the Double Four-Patch blocks.

1. Arrange the dark green, brown, and burgundy 1½" x 42" strips into eight sets of six strips each, varying the color placement in each strip set. Sew the strip sets together and carefully press the seam allowances open. I recommend using spray starch or sizing at this step to help keep the strips straight and stabilized throughout the piecing process.

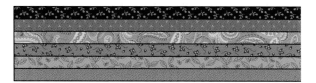

Make 8 strip sets.

2. Make a guide for cutting the Roman Stripe triangle by drawing an 8⅞" square on freezer paper or template plastic. Draw a line from corner to corner diagonally and cut out the resulting triangles. Repeat to cut six or eight triangles

if you're using freezer paper; you can re-use each one several times.

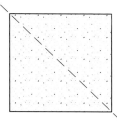

CHECK YOUR RULER STASH

If you have one of those half-square-triangle rulers that goes up to the number 8 along the side, you can use that to cut triangles from the strip sets. No cutting guide or template needed! Simply place the long edge of the triangle ruler along the edge of the strip set and cut around the two short sides with your rotary cutter.

3. Press the freezer-paper triangles to the strip sets and cut the Roman Stripe triangles as shown using the freezer-paper triangles or a triangle ruler as a cutting guide. If you're using template plastic, draw around the triangle and cut on the drawn lines. You should be able to cut five triangles from each strip set. Cut 40 triangles.

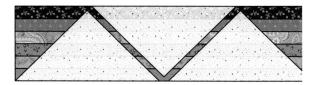

4. Sew two matching pink 2½" squares to two matching dark print 2½" squares as shown to make a four-patch unit. Make 40.

Make 40.

5. Arrange and sew two matching pink 4⅞" triangles to each four-patch unit, noting the placement of the brown squares. Press the seam allowances toward the pink triangles. Make 40.

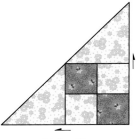

Make 40.

6. Sew a four-patch triangle to a Roman Stripe triangle to form a square block. Press the seam allowances toward the Roman Stripe. Handle the block carefully because the edges of the Roman Stripe triangle are cut on the bias. Make 40 border blocks.

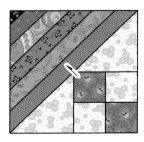

Make 40.

Assembling the Quilt Top

1. Arrange the center blocks in 10 rows of eight blocks each, carefully positioning them so that the dark squares form a chain. Rearrange blocks until you're satisfied with the placement.

2. Arrange the border blocks around the perimeter, referring to the quilt diagram above right. The Roman Stripe half of the block will create a stunning "border" around your quilt.

3. Sew the blocks together into rows. Press the seam allowances in opposite directions from row to row.

4. Sew the rows together; press the seam allowances in one direction.

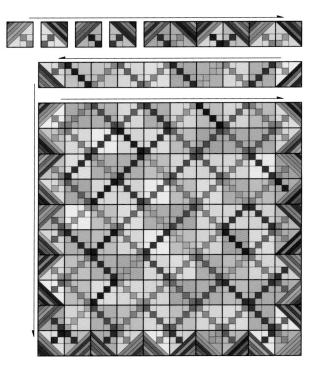

Finishing the Quilt

1. Piece the quilt backing using two horizontal seams. Layer and baste the backing, batting, and quilt top.

2. Quilt as inspired. My suggestion for this scrappy quilt is a simple allover quilting design of ribbons.

3. Prepare and attach the binding and label. Refer to "Binding Your Quilt" on page 76 if you need help with this step.

THE DRAMA CLUB

Designed and pieced by Judy Dillree, quilted by Sheila Sinclair Snyder

Finished quilt: 44½" x 44½"

Finished blocks: 12" x 12"

Materials

Yardage requirements are based on 42"-wide fabric.

4 fat quarters of assorted dark prints for block backgrounds

⅞ yard of dark print for block backgrounds

9 fat eighths of assorted orange prints for flower petals

9 fat eighths of assorted green prints for leaves

9 assorted scraps (at least 8" square) of gold or brown prints for flower centers

⅝ yard of orange hand-dyed solid for pieced sashing and border

⅝ yard of dark rust solid for pieced sashing and border

½ yard of dark print for cornerstones and binding

2⅞ yards of fabric for backing

50" x 50" piece of batting

Template plastic, at least 12" x 14"

Cutting

Read "Preparing the Templates and Cutting the Appliques" at right before you cut.

From the dark print for block backgrounds, cut *a total of*:
5 squares, 13" x 13"

From *each* of the assorted dark print fat quarters, cut:
1 square, 13" x 13"

From *each* of the assorted orange print fat eighths, cut:
1 set of 5 flower petals using templates A, B, B reversed, C, and C reversed

From *each* of the gold or brown print scraps, cut:
1 flower center using template D

From *each* of the assorted green print fat eighths, cut:
1 pair of leaves using templates E and E reversed

From the orange hand-dyed solid, cut:
11 strips, 1½" x 42"

From the dark rust solid, cut:
11 strips, 1½" x 42"

From the dark print for cornerstones and binding, cut:
6 strips, 2½" x 42"; crosscut 1 strip into 16 squares, 2½" x 2½"

Preparing Templates and Cutting the Appliqués

Refer to "Needle-Turn Appliqué" on page 75 and make a template out of template plastic for each appliqué shape. Patterns for the templates are on pages 62 and 63. Label each template and mark the back of templates B, C, and E as *reverse.* Cut the appliqués as directed in "Needle-Turn Appliqué," following the cutting list for the number to cut.

Appliquéing the Blocks

1. Position the appliqué shapes on the background block referring to the placement guide. Baste in place with thread, or pin baste with appliqué pins to secure.

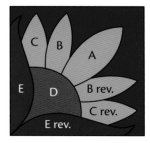

Placement guide

I like to think of these blossoms as "snapshots"—extreme close-ups, each vying for your attention and demanding that you choose a favorite! If you need some drama in your life, create your own "Drama Club" with vivid color and fanciful quilting.

2. Appliqué the shapes in sequence, working from the C and C reversed petals to the B petals, and then the A petal. Appliqué the flower center, and then the leaves.

3. Lay the block right side down on a cushioned surface and press.

4. Repeat steps 1–3 to make a total of nine blocks. Don't trim the blocks until after the sashing and border units have been made.

A BIT ABOUT THE BORDER

To let the flowers take center stage, the pieced border is simply a pieced sashing—a bold and punchy checkerboard. The trick to getting it to fit is to piece all of the sashing and border units, measure their length, and then trim all the appliqué blocks to that same dimension. Whether going horizontal or vertical, the sashing and border units will fit perfectly.

Preparing the Sashing and Border Units

1. Sew an orange 1½"-wide strip to a dark rust 1½"-wide strip. Press the seam allowances toward the rust. Make a total of 11 strip sets and crosscut them into 288 segments, 1½" wide.

1½"

Make 11 strip sets.
Cut 288 segments.

2. Arrange and sew 12 segments together, alternating the colors, to make a checkerboard strip. Press all the seam allowances in one direction. Make 24 checkerboard strips.

Make 24.

3. Measure the length of the checkerboard strips. They should measure 12½" long. If they don't, measure several and determine the average length. Square up the appliqué blocks to that size so your sashing and borders will fit perfectly.

Assembling the Quilt Top

1. Arrange the blocks, checkerboard strips, and cornerstones into rows, as shown. Rearrange the blocks until you're satisfied with the color placement.

2. Sew the blocks and checkerboard strips into rows. Sew the checkerboard strips and cornerstones into rows. Press the seam allowances toward the blocks and cornerstones.

3. Sew the rows together. Press the seam allowances all in one direction.

Finishing the Quilt

1. Piece the backing fabric using a vertical seam and trim to approximately 52" x 52". Layer and baste the backing, batting, and quilt top.

2. Quilt as inspired—with flare!

3. Prepare and attach the binding and label. Refer to "Binding Your Quilt" on page 76 if you need help with this step.

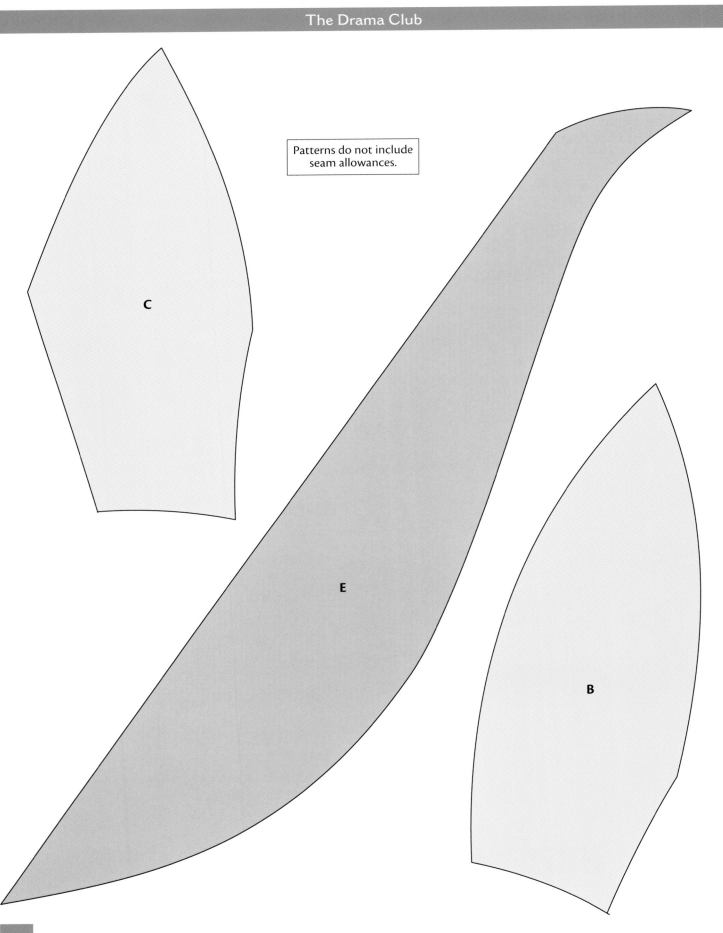

Patterns do not include
seam allowances.

C

E

B

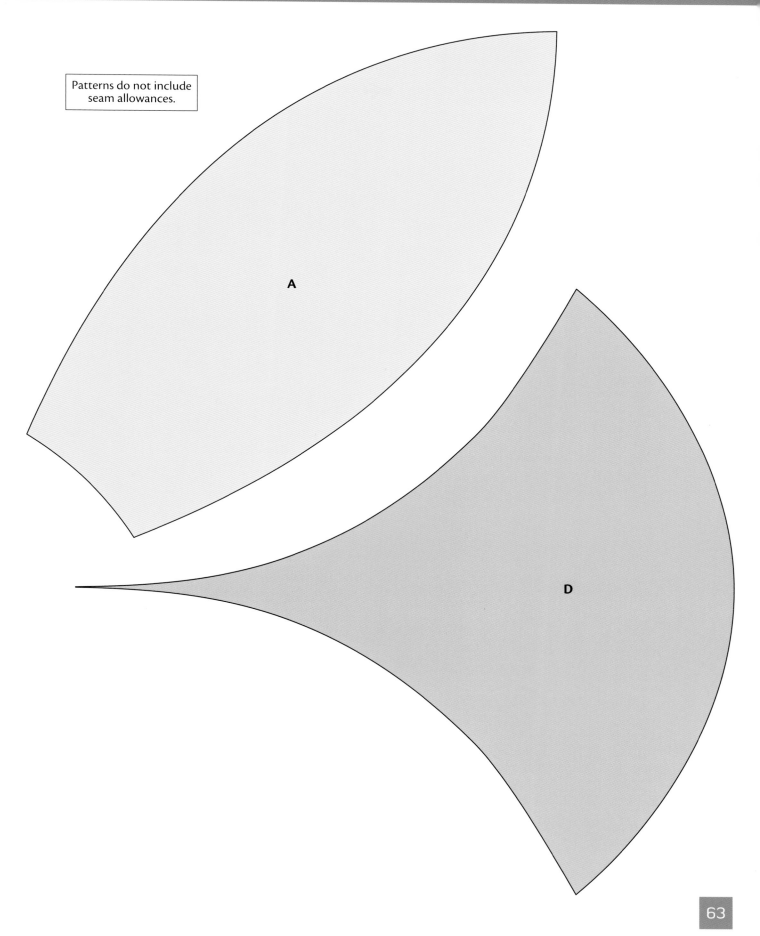

Patterns do not include seam allowances.

A

D

TULIPS TO GO

Appliqué by Yolaine Adams, Margaret Wells, Arlene Albright, Carol Gunderson and Pené Ballini, piecing and quilting by Sheila Sinclair Snyder

Finished quilt: 66½" x 66½"
Finished appliqué blocks: 15" x 15"
Finished border blocks: 3" x 3"

Materials

Yardage requirements are based on 42"-wide fabric.

4 yards of dark print for block backgrounds

2⅝ yards of bright blue print for basket handles, border blocks, and binding

1⅛ yards of large-scale orange print for baskets

1 yard of bright pink print for tulips

⅞ yard of a green print 1 for border blocks

½ yard of green print 2 for leaves

8½ yards of rickrack for tulip stems

4¼ yards of fabric for backing

73" x 73" piece of batting

12" x 18" piece of clear template plastic

½ yard of clear upholstery vinyl for overlay

5½ yards of 18"-wide fusible web such as Lite Steam-A-Seam 2

Seed beads, approximately 800 (50 per block)

Cutting

All cutting instructions include ¼"- wide seam allowances. Be sure to decide what appliqué method you will use and read "Preparing the Appliqués and Overlay" on page 66 before cutting the appliqué pieces.

From the dark print, cut*:
16 squares, 15½" x 15½"

From the large-scale orange print, cut:
16 baskets using template A

From the bright blue print, cut:
16 basket handles using template B

9 strips, 2⅜" x 42", crosscut into 144 squares, 2⅜" x 2⅜"

3 strips, 4½" x 42, crosscut into 24 squares, 4½" x 4½"; cut each square into quarters diagonally to yield 96 triangles

7 binding strips, 2" x 42"

From green print 2, cut:
16 leaves using template C
16 leaves using template D

From the bright pink print, cut:
16 of *each* tulip piece using templates E, F, G, H, I, J, K

From green print 1, cut:
3 strips, 3½" x 42", crosscut into 36 squares, 3½" x 3½".

3 strips, 4½" x 42", crosscut into 24 squares, 4½" x 4½"; cut each square into quarters diagonally to yield 96 triangles

From the rickrack, cut:
16 pieces, 6½" long
16 pieces, 2½" long
16 pieces, 8" long

* If you prefer to do needle-turn appliqué, cut your blocks ½" larger to accommodate for any uptake or shrinkage that occurs while you appliqué. This is not necessary when using fusible web.

Ethlyn Pearson, a talented writer and colorful family member, told me a story as she was giving me a tattered quilt. The quilt had been made for her when she graduated from high school. Her mother, grandmother, and aunts had each contributed fabrics and worked together to create a hand-appliquéd tulip-basket quilt. Ethlyn is now in her mid-eighties and has loved that quilt well. In fact, so well that it's falling apart! I realized it was beyond repair and used it as inspiration for a new quilt. So, here's to you, Aunt Ethlyn, a contemporary version of your beloved quilt, completed by a group of women sitting around my dining-room table.

Preparing the Appliqués and Overlay

The instructions are written for fusible appliqué. If you want to do hand appliqué, refer to "Needle-Turn Appliqué" for additional information as needed and reverse the templates when tracing.

1. Using the patterns on pages 71–73, and a fine-point permanent marker, trace each shape onto clear template plastic following the solid lines. Label each template with a letter and a notation for the front. Dashed lines on the patterns represent areas of overlap.

2. Cut out the templates on the drawn line.

3. Trace each template onto the paper side of the fusible web, leaving at least ½" between shapes. If you're using double-stick fusible web, trace onto the front paper, according to the manufacturer's instructions. You'll need 16 of each piece.

4. Loosely cut around the appliqué shapes, approximately ¼" from the drawn lines. For multiple shapes, you can cut around the entire grouping.

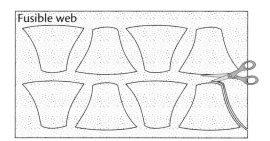
Fusible web

5. Following the manufacturer's instructions and referring to the cutting list, place the fusible web onto the *wrong* side of the appropriate fabrics. Fuse or lightly press in place as directed for your fusible product.

6. Cut out the shapes on the solid lines.

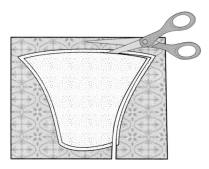

7. Enlarge the block diagram on page 74 using a photocopier to make a full-size diagram for tracing. You may need to tape sheets of paper together after copying.

8. Cut the upholstery vinyl into a 16" x 16" square. It will cut easily with scissors or a rotary cutter.

9. Use a fine-point permanent marker to trace the full-size Tulip Basket block design onto the vinyl overlay. Include the seam line, as this will be used to center the overlay onto the background fabric. Label the front of the overlay so that you don't accidentally flip it upside down.

designer's tip:
EASY APPLIQUÉ PLACEMENT

Whenever you're making several of the same appliquéd blocks, make and use a vinyl overlay. This will enable you to accurately place each shape very quickly. When you're finished with yours, share it with a friend!

Making the Appliqué Blocks

1. Place a background square on your ironing board or pressing surface. Place the vinyl overlay on top and pin or weigh it down to hold it in place. Now you're ready to slip each appliqué piece under the overlay into perfect position.

2. Position the basket, followed by the handle, tucking the ends of the handle under the edge of the basket.

3. Add the leaves, tucking leaf C under leaf D.

4. Position the lower tulip starting with piece E and covering it with piece F.

5. Position the center tulip with piece G under piece H.

6. Position the right tulip starting with piece I, adding piece J, and finishing with piece K.

7. Add the 6½" piece of rickrack to the left tulip, tucking the ends under the tulip and under the basket following the overlay. Add the 2½" piece of rickrack to the center tulip, tucking the ends under the tulip and leaves. Add the 8" piece of rickrack to the right tulip in the same manner.

8. Remove the vinyl overlay. Following the manufacturer's instructions, fuse the appliqué onto the background. The rickrack will be stabilized at each end, but will remain loose until a later step.

9. Repeat steps 1–8 to make 16 blocks.

Make 16.

Finishing the Appliqué Blocks

1. Stitch around each motif using a blanket stitch to give it a finished look. You may choose to do this by hand, or use your sewing machine as I did. I had fun using variegated threads for the basket, leaves, and tulips; for the basket handle, I stayed with a solid color. Begin by stitching the handle, then the leaves, basket, and flowers.

HAND BLANKET STITCH

To hand stitch the edges of your appliqués, use a needle that will accommodate two or three strands of embroidery floss, or number 8 pearl cotton. Knot the thread and bring the needle up in the background fabric at A next to the edge of the appliqué. Working toward yourself, insert the needle into the appliqué at B and up in the background at C, keeping the thread underneath the needle.

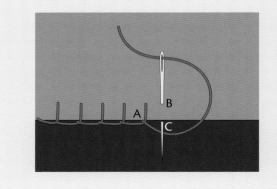

2. Stitch the tulip stems in place and add embellishment at the same time by using seed beads. Space the beads approximately ¼" apart along the rickrack and use the beading to help you manipulate the rickrack into a nice smooth line. I was lucky to find a velvet rickrack that added additional texture. You may also use embroidery to attach your rickrack. Stitches such as French knot, herringbone, featherstitch, chevron stitch, and lazy daisy would attach and add embellishment as well.

designer's tip:
EASY BEADING

I started out using a beading needle to add the seed beads, but soon found out they're nearly impossible to thread, and they're very weak. After some experimentation, I found that a regular sewing needle, size 11, was much easier for me to use and the bead slipped over it just fine. I used regular cotton thread for this task, and it was easy to find a color to match the beads.

Making the Hourglass Blocks

The squares and triangles for these blocks were cut oversized. The blocks will be trimmed after sewing to ensure accuracy in the final size.

1. Sew each green triangle to a blue triangle as shown, carefully keeping a consistent color on top as you sew each pair. Press the seam allowances toward the lighter fabric. Make 96 units.

Make 96.

2. Sew two units together, matching the center seam. Press the seam allowances in one direction. Make 48 blocks.

Make 48.

3. Square up the blocks to 3½" x 3½" using a square ruler. Align the 45° line of your ruler with the diagonal seam line of the block, and place the intersection of 1¾" lines of your ruler on the block center. Cut along the right and top sides. Rotate the block and align the 3½" lines of your ruler with the trimmed sides of the block. Cut the right and top sides of the block and you'll have a 3½" square Hourglass block.

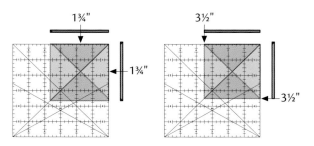

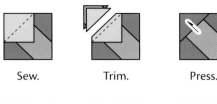

A BIT ABOUT THE BORDER

I created this border design to resemble a woven basket handle. It's made up of two simple blocks, pieced together in units that correspond to the basket block dimensions. You'll get a big bang for your piecing bucks with this striking border.

Making the Square-in-a-Square Blocks

I modified the traditional Square-in-a-Square block so that the center square is smaller and will float inside the block rather than touch the outside seam allowances. This gives the border a more dimensional look. It also has the benefit of reducing bulk in the seam allowance.

1. Mark the wrong side of each blue 2⅜" square with a diagonal line from corner to corner.

2. Place a marked blue square on the corner of a green 3½" square, right sides together, as shown. Sew along the drawn line on the blue square. Trim the seam allowances to ¼" and press the seam allowances toward the corner. Repeat on the opposite corner.

Sew. Trim. Press.

Sew. Trim. Press.

3. Sew a blue square to each of the remaining corners of the green square. Trim the seam allowances and press toward the corner. The block should measure 3½" x 3½". Make 36 blocks.

Sew. Trim. Press.

Sew. Trim. Press. Make 36.

Assembling the Quilt Top

1. Sew three Hourglass blocks and two Square-in-a-Square blocks together as shown. Press the seam allowances in one direction. Make 16 border units. There will be four Square-in-a-Square blocks remaining.

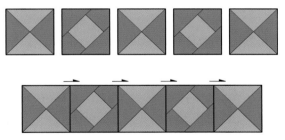

Make 16.

2. Arrange the Basket blocks in four rows of four blocks each, alternating the orientation as shown below. Add the border units to the top and bottom in rows, and to the sides of each basket row. Add a Square-in-a-Square block to each corner of the quilt to complete the border design.

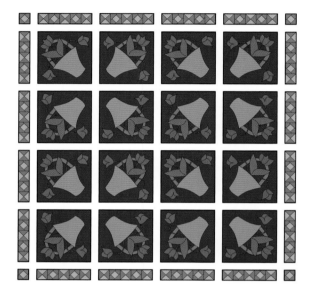

3. Sew the blocks and border units together into rows. Press the seam allowances in opposite directions from row to row.

4. Sew the rows together; press the seam allowances all in one direction.

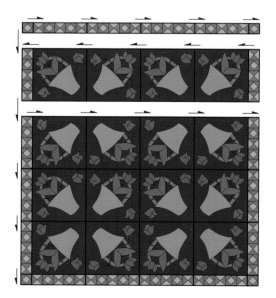

Finishing the Quilt

1. Piece the quilt backing using a vertical seam. Layer and baste the backing, batting, and quilt top.

2. Quilt as inspired. I enjoyed developing a custom design for this quilt in the areas between the basket bottoms. It may seem complicated, but there's simply a lot of variety in the scale of the fun curlicue motifs. I used four different thread colors when stitching the background, border, and open spaces between the blocks.

3. Prepare and attach the binding and label. Refer to "Binding Your Quilt" on page 76 if you need help with this step.

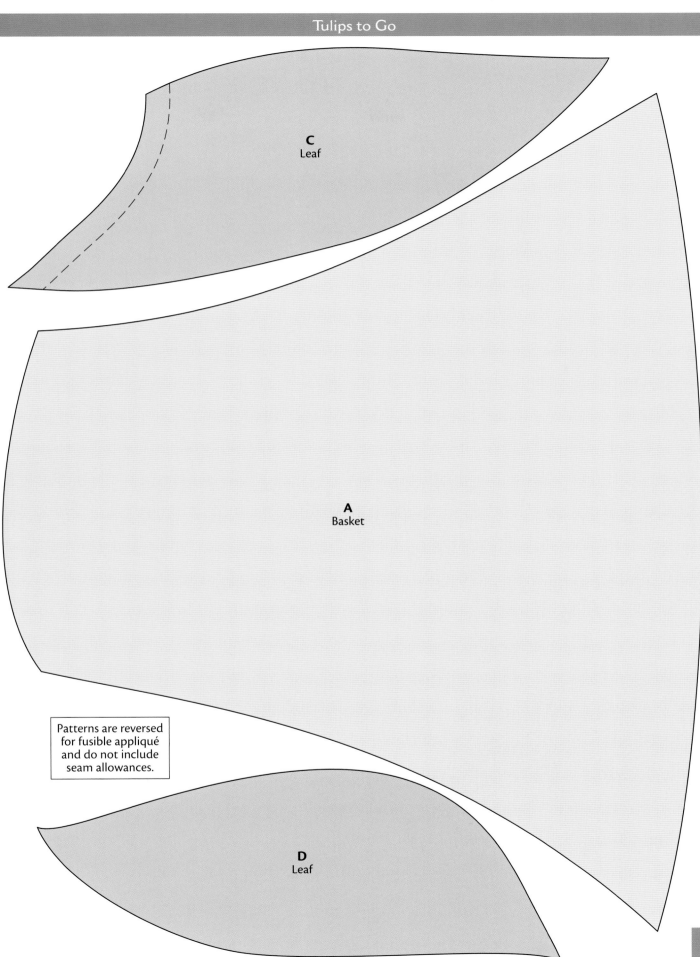

C
Leaf

A
Basket

Patterns are reversed
for fusible appliqué
and do not include
seam allowances.

D
Leaf

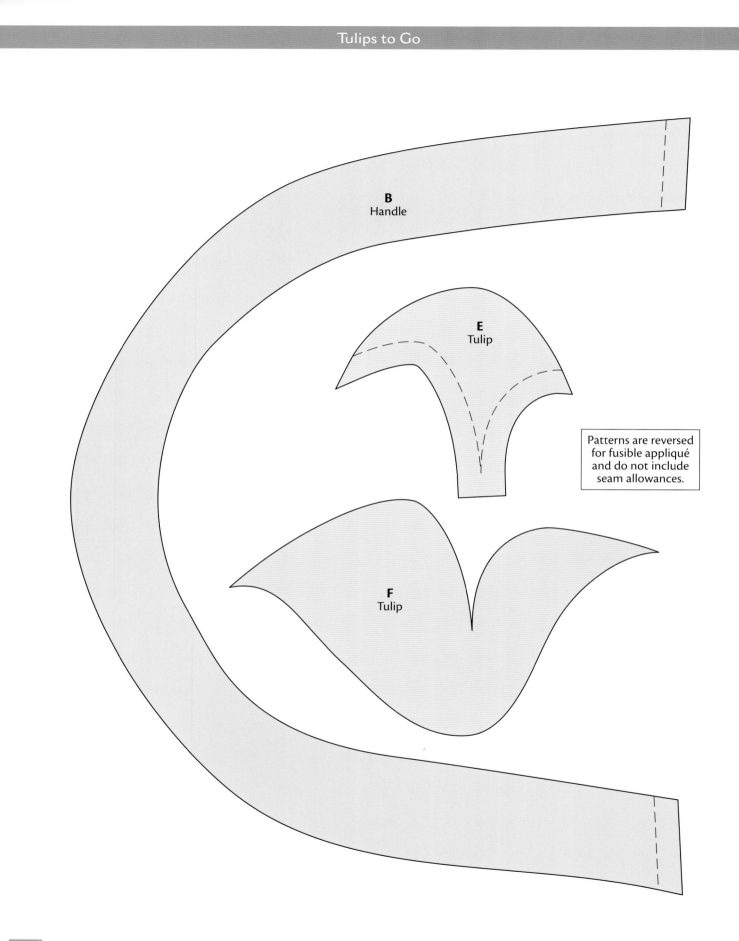

B
Handle

E
Tulip

Patterns are reversed
for fusible appliqué
and do not include
seam allowances.

F
Tulip

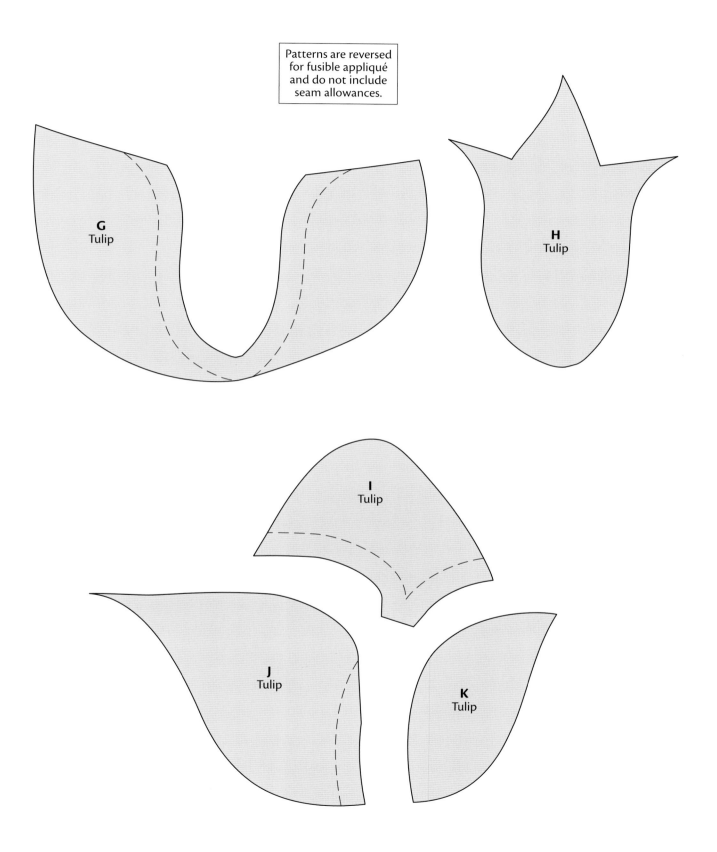

Patterns are reversed
for fusible appliqué
and do not include
seam allowances.

G
Tulip

H
Tulip

I
Tulip

J
Tulip

K
Tulip

Block diagram
Enlarge 200%.

This section provides some basic instructions for the hand appliqué method that I use, in addition to binding and finishing instructions. If you are a beginner, check out some of the many excellent books on quiltmaking for additional information.

Needle-Turn Appliqué

Needle-turn appliqué is a time-honored method of appliquéing by hand and using your needle to turn under the seam allowance as you sew.

1. Trace the entire appliqué pattern onto stiff paper. The dull side of a sheet of freezer paper makes an excellent choice. If you'll be using or tracing the template many times, you may want to use template plastic available at quilt shops, fabric stores, and craft stores. Transfer any center horizontal and vertical lines to use as registration marks for placing the appliqué onto the background fabric.

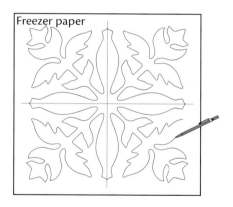

Freezer paper

2. Cut out the pattern directly on the traced lines.

3. Position the pattern on the right side of the desired appliqué fabric. Press the freezer paper in place using a dry iron. Trace the pattern onto the fabric with a water-soluble marker or a mechanical pencil. This line marks the edge you'll turn under and stitch. Avoid using a chalk marker for this task, as it will not withstand the repeated handling needed and will wear off too quickly.

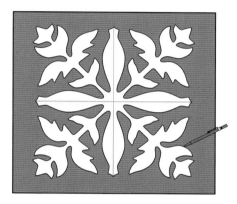

4. Roughly cut out the fabric shape, allowing a generous ¼" seam allowance. You'll trim the seam allowance further during the appliqué process.

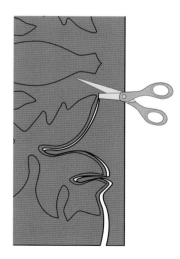

5. Prepare the background fabric by folding it in half vertically, and then in half again. Press gently to mark the fold lines and center point.

Note that the background piece is cut slightly oversized to compensate for any drawing up that may occur as you stitch.

6. Position the appliqué piece onto the background fabric, matching the centers and any other registration marks. Baste the appliqué in place.

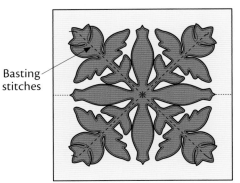

Basting stitches

7. Thread a sharp, fine needle with a single strand of thread that matches the color of the appliqué piece. Knot the thread at one end. Choose a place to begin on the appliqué piece. (A straight edge or gentle curve makes a good place to start.) You'll work a small section at a time. Roll the edge of the appliqué fabric under to hide the marked stitching line. Finger-press and trim the seam allowance if necessary.

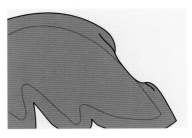

8. Bring your needle from the wrong side of the background fabric to the front, catching just a few threads on the rolled edge of the appliqué. Pull the thread through completely. Re-enter the background fabric next to the point where the needle emerged from the appliqué piece and slightly under the rolled edge.

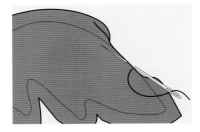

9. Repeat the basic stitch, working your way around the outline of the appliqué shape. The stitches should be approximately ⅛" apart or less, especially for intricate shapes and turns. Pull the thread so that the appliqué lies flat against the background but does not pucker. Trim the seam allowances as needed and turn the edge of the appliqué piece under with the needle as you sew. Clip the curves and points as you go.

10. Finish by making two tiny stitches on the back of the block. Take a third stitch and pull the needle through the loop to make a knot. Remove the basting and any remaining visible markings. Square up the block to the correct size as indicated in the project instructions.

Layering multiple appliqué shapes onto each other is a fun way to add dimension to your quilts; take special care to tuck the shapes into each other as needed. You may need to stitch an appliqué piece in stages, inserting and layering other pieces as you go before finishing the original shape.

Binding Your Quilt

A well-chosen and well-applied binding gives your quilt a nicely finished edge. I typically use a double-fold binding made from 2"-wide strips. I choose this size because I like the look of a narrow finished binding, and because the size feels right in my hands as I'm working.

1. Cut the number of binding strips as directed in the project instructions. (The required number of strips can be determined by totaling the length of all four sides of the quilt, adding approximately 10" for turning corners and for seams, and dividing the total by 40", the approximate width of the fabric).

2. Piece the binding strips together end to end with angled seams as shown to minimize bulk. Press the seam allowances open.

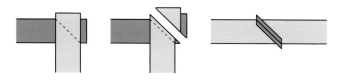

3. Press the binding in half lengthwise, wrong sides together. Cut one end of the binding at a 45° angle, fold under ½", and press firmly to crease.

Fold line

4. Trim the excess batting and backing even with the edge of the quilt top.

5. Align the raw edges of the folded binding with the raw edges of the quilt top. Beginning several inches from a corner and approximately 5" or more from the angled end of the binding, sew the binding to the quilt using a scant ¼" seam allowance. If your binding strips are wider or narrower than 2", you may need to adjust the seam allowance slightly.

6. Stop stitching ¼" from the first corner of the quilt and backstitch. Remove the quilt from the machine.

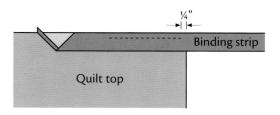

¼"

Binding strip

Quilt top

7. Fold the binding straight up as shown, parallel with the next edge of the quilt. Fold the binding down along this edge to form a pleat, aligning the folded edge of the binding even with the top raw edge of the quilt.

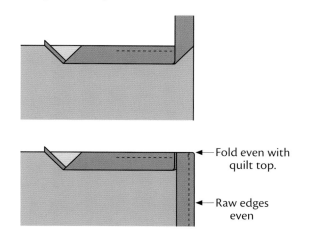

Fold even with quilt top.

Raw edges even

8. Continue stitching the binding, turning corners as described. Stop stitching approximately 10" to 12" from the starting point of the binding and backstitch. Remove the quilt from the machine.

9. Lay the remaining unbound edge of the quilt on a flat surface. Unfold both ends of the binding strip. Fold the end of the strip and butt it against the starting end of the strip as shown. Press the crease.

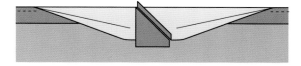

10. Pull the binding away from the quilt and join the strips with machine or hand stitching using the pressed creases as the stitching line.

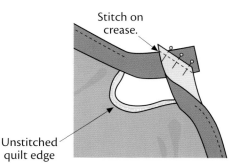

Stitch on crease.

Unstitched quilt edge

11. Check that the binding length is correct. Trim the seam allowances to ¼" and press the seam allowances open.

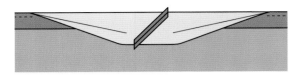

12. Complete the seam to attach the remaining binding to the quilt.

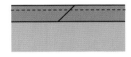

13. Fold the binding to the back of the quilt. A miter will form at each corner. Secure the binding on the back with a blind stitch or hemstitch so that the folded edge covers the machine-stitching line. Take a stitch or two in each corner to secure the mitered folds in place on both the front and back of the quilt.

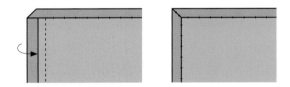

Making a Removable Hanging Sleeve

You never know when you'll want to display your quilt on a wall or at a show. Be ready with this quilt-friendly method of hanging your quilt. Since it's not sewn into the binding, you can remove the sleeve at any time.

1. Cut a strip of fabric 8" by the width of your quilt. You may need to sew strips together to get the needed length.

2. Turn and press under a ½" hem on each end of the strip. Repeat and stitch the hem.

½" ½"

3. Fold the strip in half lengthwise, right sides together. Sew the strip into a long tube using ¼" seam allowance. Turn the tube right side out and press flat.

4. Slip-stitch the top edge of the sleeve to the quilt backing just below the binding. Slip-stitch the bottom edge of the hanging sleeve to the quilt backing.

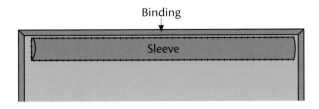

Binding

Sleeve

Adding a Label

It's very important to label each quilt. A label gives you an opportunity to document the quilt for the future and to include a sentiment if you choose. I often piece my label into the backing of the quilt; the quilting ensures that the label won't come off. Other times I appliqué the label to the backing after the quilt is finished.

Be sure your label includes the name of the quilt; the name of the maker; the city, state, and date; and—if possible—the name of the quilter and the recipient. Include any other information to help document the quilt.

Labels can be embroidered, cross-stitched, printed on the computer, written with permanent fabric markers, or any combination of the above. Be creative in adding this finishing touch to your quilt!

ABOUT THE AUTHOR

When not teaching, designing, writing books, or making quilts, you'll likely find Sheila tearing apart the kitchen for a remodel or painting the house! An award-winning long-arm quilter, Sheila always enjoys having a project going and tends to start thinking about the next one before the current one is finished! The designs keep coming, the ideas continue to flow, and she couldn't stop if she tried.

THERE'S MORE ONLINE!

Check Sheila's website (www.licensetoquilt.com) for her current teaching schedule, and feel free to contact her at sheila@licensetoquilt.com. Find more great books on quilting, sewing, and more at www.martingale-pub.com.